Human Rights

The Case for the Defence

SHAMI CHAKRABARTI

PENGUIN BOOKS

PENGUIN BOOKS

UK | USA | Canada | Ireland | Australia
India | New Zealand | South Africa

Penguin Books is part of the Penguin Random House group of companies whose addresses can be found at global.penguinrandomhouse.com.

Penguin Random House UK,
One Embassy Gardens, 8 Viaduct Gardens, London SW11 7BW

penguin.co.uk

First published by Allen Lane 2024
Published with a new Preface in Penguin Books 2025
003

Typeset by Jouve (UK), Milton Keynes

Printed and bound in Great Britain by Clays Ltd, Elcograf S.p.A.

The authorized representative in the EEA is Penguin Random House Ireland, Morrison Chambers, 32 Nassau Street, Dublin D02 YH68

A CIP catalogue record for this book is available from the British Library

ISBN: 978–1–802–06091–1

Penguin Random House is committed to a sustainable future for our business, our readers and our planet. This book is made from Forest Stewardship Council® certified paper.

PENGUIN BOOKS

Human Rights

'The threat to human rights is ever increasing and the practical way this book informs us is commendable. The book gives us a road map of what we are facing that is easy to understand. People across the world face more conflict than ever. Wars that have nothing to do with ordinary people going about their daily lives come from the governments that are supposed to protect them. The book is worth reading' Doreen Lawrence

'A book that is as passionate, as precise, as needed, as human rights themselves. After 30 years as a lawyer and campaigner at the rock-face of human rights work, Shami Chakrabarti argues the case for defending and promoting these rights with reason, lyricism and subtlety, offering us comfort and a compass for the future' Ahdaf Soueif

'I would follow this woman to the end of the earth. If you are a human you need to read Shami Chakrabati's *Human Rights*. If you are not then don't. We need this book now more than ever' Lemn Sissay

'Human rights need informed and passionate supporters, perhaps now more than ever. Shami Chakrabarti is both, her eloquence and persuasiveness evident in every page of this lively and accessible book' Conor Gearty

'At once primer and urgent clarion call, Shami Chakrabarti's brilliant history and defence of human rights could not have come at a better time. Lucid, exacting and passionate, this book is required reading for critics and advocates alike. Chakrabarti reminds us that rights are not there to make us comfortable, and nor should they be traded for political points. Rights exist to keep us – and our democracies – free' Lyndsey Stonebridge

'Chakrabarti's bracing defence of human rights against their sceptics is as accessible as it is necessary. Connecting historical struggles for justice under law with today's challenges on a burning and war-torn planet, she has made another indispensable contribution to our public life' Samuel Moyn

'In a world which increasingly threatens the rights and values many of us have come to take for granted, Chakrabarti's book is a timely reminder of both the history of these hard won freedoms and how they have come to shape what a just and fair society looks like. Her powerful, important book reminds us why we must continue to hold human rights up to the light, ensuring they protect not only the human dignity of the most vulnerable but the health and strength of a democratic society' Sarah Langford

'Absorbing . . . a useful primer for the layperson, explaining the basic rights and principles underlying the sort of morally complex arguments – over free speech on university campuses, or whether the famously strict Michaela school can ban pupils from praying, or whether Israel has committed war crimes in Gaza, or whether a Christian baker can be fairly expected to bake someone a wedding cake for a same-sex couple – that keep hitting the headlines . . . For Chakrabarti the ECHR isn't just a set of amalgamated legal safeguards but a source of "sheer poetic insight" into human nature . . . there is a hidden beauty in it' Gaby Hinsliff, *Observer*

'A timely and forcefully argued case for the defence of human rights . . . On its own, the book's introduction is a pleasure to read and would draw any reader in to want to understand more about the immediate questions relating to human rights that need answers now. It can't be left to experts, whether legal, academic or political. Anyone casting a vote . . . needs to understand the debate on human rights as it is central to so many current political decisions' Pauline Bryan, *The House Magazine*

'Full of passion and idealism but also fine scholarship, this book sets out a plan for how Humanity can avoid a cruel, Hobbesian future. It will be required reading for anyone who believes that Human Rights offer a better path forward for global society than the Manichean one it is presently treading' Andrew Roberts

ABOUT THE AUTHOR

Shami Chakrabarti is a leading British human rights lawyer and campaigner who has written and broadcast widely and held a number of public roles in recent decades. A legislator in the House of Lords, she is the author of *On Liberty* and *Of Women*. Director of Liberty (the National Council for Civil Liberties) from 2003 to 2016, she was Shadow Attorney General for England and Wales from 2016 to 2020.

In memory of
Shyamali and Mintoo Chakrabarti

There may be those who would like to live in a country where these rights are not protected but I am not of their number.

Tom Bingham

Contents

Preface

The turbulence of the times into which this book was born has only intensified. Around half the people on the planet live in more than seventy countries that held national polls in 2024, the largest election year in history. A theme of 2024 was the punishment of incumbents. In many places, there was also a rise in far-right populism, highlighting a contradiction at the heart of even notionally free elections. Without constant vigilance and energetic defence of rights, freedoms and the rule of law, democracy is capable of voting itself out of existence.

In numbers of eligible voters, the United States ranked third behind India and the European Parliament. However, after being the most closely watched contest, it may well prove to be the most globally significant. There is no avoiding the challenge to the values in these pages as the forty-fifth US President becomes the forty-seventh.

Within twenty days of re-election and just under two months before his scheduled inauguration, Donald Trump celebrated the dropping of all federal criminal charges against him. These related to election interference and the appropriation of classified documents after losing the 2020 race. The US Department of Justice (DOJ) interprets the Constitution as implicitly prohibiting any prosecution of a sitting President. Without irony, a Trump spokesperson hailed the DOJ announcement as a 'major victory for the rule of law'. Whatever one's views on Trumpian politics or the substance of the indictments, it is hard to square such a blanket practical immunity (going beyond even protection for 'official' acts) with equality before the law.

At the other end of unequal treatment, if Trump's first term is anything to go by, a whole host of groups within and beyond the borders of the Republic have significant cause for concern. Under Trump I, several Muslim and African countries faced US travel bans, and migrants – including children – at the US border endured a host of cruelties. Women's reproductive rights were first rolled back by international aid policy and later domestically, by the overturning of *Roe v Wade* in *Dobbs v Jackson Women's Health Organization* by a Supreme Court including three Trump-nominated justices. Advocates for unfettered freedom are invariably selective in its application.

If nationalism, isolationism and deregulation are to exemplify US policy once more, this brings serious implications for conflicts in Russia and Ukraine and the Middle East in particular. It also weakens the ability of the international community and its institutions effectively to address new technologies and the existential threat of the climate emergency in the short term.

In France – another permanent member of the UN Security Council (the P5) – Marine Le Pen's Rassemblement National attracted most votes at the European elections, standing on an anti-immigration platform and advocating a 'constitutional shield' against European case law. In Germany, and elsewhere in the EU, far-right parties also gained ground at the expense of progressive and greener ones, with the German elections in 2025 following the collapse of Chancellor Scholz's government serving as a litmus test for the strength of the trend. Longer-term implications for wider EU policy remain to be seen.

In the United Kingdom, Labour returned to power after fourteen years with explicit commitments to human rights and the rule of law. However, Reform UK – the successor party to UKIP and the Brexit Party – gained 14.3 per cent of the vote and a parliamentary foothold (if disproportionately low compared to vote share) of five seats. Labour's honeymoon was further dampened by days of racist violent disorder in parts of England and Northern Ireland, ostensibly targeted at asylum seekers and their lawyers. Social media played a significant role in fomenting and coordinating the violence. Elon Musk, the world's richest man, subsequently appointed to the new Trump administration, was an open instigator, posting remarks that 'civil war is inevitable'. 2025 brought a further escalation of his war of words against the UK Government.

By contrast, tens of thousands of ordinary Britons engaged in community clean-up operations and counter-protests in the days and months that followed. They demonstrated solidarity with those seeking refuge in our country and undoubtedly saw off further disturbances in many towns and cities.

A criminal justice system undermined by years of cuts and neglect swung into action to prioritise the disorder. Two hundred people were sentenced (most to imprisonment) within around two months of the cessation of the riots. This was greeted with charges of 'two-tier' policing by Reform's Nigel Farage and even some mainstream British Conservative voices. I believe accelerated due process to be necessary to restoring law and order in such circumstances. However, 'necessary is not sufficient'. If the rule of law is to endure in a country so proud of its legal traditions, people led astray by alienation, inequality, misinformation and far-right manipulation need to see law that protects as well as prosecutes them. They need to own, understand and be able to access their rights in practice, whether against neglectful public services and governments or unscrupulous landlords, employers and retail corporations.

Also in the UK, the Post Office Horizon IT scandal is a case in point. Between 1999 and 2015, the Post Office had pursued thousands of innocent sub-postmasters for alleged financial shortfalls that were in fact caused by faults in the Horizon accounting software developed by the Japanese multinational corporation Fujitsu. These were small, often family-run businesses serving their local communities, but under extremely onerous contracts with the state-owned post office company. A combination of byzantine and unaccountable governance arrangements and blind trust in the infallibility of the software allowed Post Office executives and lawyers to bring abusive civil claims and criminal prosecutions against sub-postmasters for theft, fraud and false accounting. More than 900 were convicted and others were forced to cover supposed shortfalls from their own savings. The loss of homes, businesses and freedom followed, alongside bankruptcies, family breakdowns and at least four suicides in one of the greatest miscarriages of justice in modern United Kingdom history.

After dogged campaigning by former sub-postmaster Alan Bates and others, alongside expensive and often soul-destroying litigation, convictions began to be quashed in court, rendering those affected and others eligible for compensation. In May 2024, Parliaments in London and Edinburgh legislated to overturn convictions en masse. In contrast with, say, the infamous Safety of Rwanda Act 2024, the Post Office (Horizon System) Offences Act 2024 and its Scottish counterpart responded in keeping with senior judicial findings about wrongful convictions. Secondly, again in contrast with the Rwanda scheme, the new law worked in favour of vulnerable individuals and not against them. Thirdly, executive criminal pardons (as opposed to immunities) are well established in rule of law-based systems. Parliamentary authorisation is arguably far more legitimate than executive fiat. In any event, it is to be hoped that this scandal will be remembered whenever we are sold inscrutable and unaccountable technological systems likely to impact upon our liberties and lives.

Furthermore, recent events in the field of artificial intelligence (AI), in the context of war and in environmental policy have demonstrated the essential nature of human rights thinking as a guide to our shared future. In the context of artificial intelligence regulation, the EU and the US chose markedly different paths even before President Trump's re-election. The EU AI Act came into force in August 2024. It takes an active regulatory approach to the technology based on varying levels of risk, thus establishing the EU as a global leader in the field.

By contrast, the Biden administration opted for an industry-led approach with its Executive Order on the Safe, Secure, and Trustworthy Development and Use of Artificial Intelligence, relying on voluntary standards and collaboration with the private sector. It resembles a statement of principle and international intent, rather than hard-edged regulation.

This may be unsurprising given the wealth and influence of Silicon Valley. Trump's appointment of a tech billionaire to the new Department of Government Efficiency with its cost, regulation and bureaucracy-cutting mission, as well as longstanding support from modern tech plutocrats such as Peter Thiel, will no doubt have implications for future AI policy. China's increasing prominence in AI and advanced chip technologies may also enhance tensions between superpowers in an increasingly multipolar world.

At the interface between war and law, developments in Israel and Palestine have been particularly tragic since the Hamas atrocity and mass hostage-taking of October 2023 and Israel's indiscriminate and catastrophic response in Gaza. In

December 2023, South Africa brought a claim of genocide against Israel before the International Court of Justice (ICJ). This was supported by over thirty other states and international organisations, mostly in the Global South. Supporters also include P5 member and human rights-sceptical China, and Ireland, Slovenia, Spain and Turkey within the Council of Europe.

The ongoing case prompted the court to order protective interim measures, requiring Israel to prevent acts contrary to the UN's 1948 Convention on the Prevention and Punishment of the Crime of Genocide. Later it added an order to ensure basic food supplies to Palestinians in Gaza facing famine and starvation. It also expressed concern for the Israeli hostages still being held in the Gaza Strip. It did not order the end of Israel's military campaign.

In September 2024, the UN General Assembly voted by 124 to 14 (with 43 abstentions) to adopt a resolution demanding that Israel 'brings to an end without delay its unlawful presence' in the Occupied Palestinian Territory. This was in response to an advisory opinion of illegal occupation by the ICJ that also called upon international organisations and states to cooperate to compel Israel to comply. However, in the final weeks of the US election race, this resolution prompted no significant change of approach from the flailing presidency of Israel's closest ally and potentially crucial peace-broker.

Perhaps even more dramatically, on 21 November 2024, the ICJ issued arrest warrants against Israel's Prime Minister Benjamin Netanyahu and former defence minister Yoav Gallant, alongside Hamas military commander Mohammed Deif. The judges found reasonable grounds for believing that these men bore criminal responsibility for alleged war crimes and crimes against humanity in the Israel–Hamas conflict. International controversy around these warrants revived many of the fundamental arguments about universality versus sovereignty discussed in this book.

The US and Israeli governments' vociferous rejections of the warrants appear to be based upon Israel (like the US) not being a party to the Rome Statute, which established the International Criminal Court (ICC). However, the occupied West Bank, East Jerusalem and Gaza were ruled to be within ICC jurisdiction in 2021. Another common refrain refers to 'no moral equivalence' between Israel and Hamas. However, moral equivalence with other alleged perpetrators of crimes has never been an ingredient in criminal responsibility. Were it the case, legitimate democratic leaders all over the world might be rendered effectively immune from this personal accountability.

How the leaders of 124 state parties, including the UK and various EU members, respond to the ICC warrants in the event of prospective visits by Messrs Netanyahu and Gallant is an important test for international law, particularly where state responses diverge from those to President Putin's arrest warrant in 2023. Just as important, perhaps, will be the response of popular opinion within Israel and across the democratic world.

Finally, the UN Climate Change Conference COP29 may have been a triumph of hope over resolution. It began with the host nation Azerbaijan accused of oppressing political opponents and its president describing fossil fuels as 'a gift of God'. It ended with a $300 billion finance commitment from developed to developing countries by 2035. NGOs and poorer nations agree this figure falls considerably short of that required to limit global warming to 1.5 degrees centigrade. Richer countries complain that economies such as China and Saudi Arabia are still categorised as developing and therefore not required to provide finance. Nonetheless, some close observers described new alliances between EU and small island states, and the Conference of the Parties to the Convention on Climate Change lives on alongside ambitions for new emissions targets to be agreed in 2025 at COP30 in Brazil.

I believe these developments add greater urgency to what follows, not least the argument that a rights and rules-based approach might still shape common values, language and cause in our troubled world.

Shami Chakrabarti, London, January 2025

Introduction

Dignity is indivisible . . . Without dignity our lives are only blinks of duration. But if we manage to live a good life well, we create something more. We write a subscript to our mortality. We make our lives tiny diamonds in the cosmic sands.

Ronald Dworkin[1]

To believe in human rights is to believe in human beings. It is to strive for everything we need to live with the possibility of flourishing in the world. It requires thoughtful empathy; an appreciation of our species as creatures of body and mind, of instinct, emotion, faith, logic and reason; individuals but also social beings. Humans yearn for autonomy, but also belonging and respect. These twin aspirations combine in the concept of 'dignity'. This recognizes that every human life matters and that, as far as possible, each of us should have agency in the way we live.

Human rights provide the poetry of both cries for freedom and pleas for protection. When the sacred and secular collide, each seeks this special higher ground, as do all competing interests in battles for liberty, equality, recognition and resources at home and abroad.

The world is in turmoil, ravaged by wars; real and imagined, proxy and phoney. It is riven by oppression, inequality and impending climate catastrophe. What many had come to rely on as the post-1945 settlement for securing greater justice, equality and peace is now once more in flux. This is especially, if not uniquely, so in the Middle East, and in Europe where two world wars and then the Cold War once began. However, despite all sorts of progressive advancement, global population growth and technology and weapons proliferation bring an ever-greater interconnection that makes conflict anywhere perilous for people everywhere.

As a currency of values, human rights are constantly called upon and yet still reviled. Invocation and attack may come from the same voices at different times. There are sceptics across the political spectrum. They question whether we need any higher laws, let alone fundamental rights that the powerful – whether via might, privilege or numbers – may neither bestow nor withdraw. They contest the basis of these principles, their content, limits, application and enforcement. Is it possible to agree or at least establish the ground rules of reasonable disagreement, so that human rights might survive and offer comfort and a compass for the future? I believe so. This book is my contribution to that endeavour.

Let's conduct a thought experiment. A person believes themselves to be totally alone on a new continent or planet. What good would calling for their rights do for them? Struggling in a state of isolation, each day would no doubt be extremely hard; finding water, food and shelter, fending off other creatures and the demons of a lonely mind. If they believe in a higher power, they could plead for divine assistance. But that isn't a demand for rights.

Let's say there are two people. They are in cooperation, conflict or some combination of the two. They discuss and debate the wisdom of particular courses of action, even how fairly they treat each other. These interpersonal disputes might be resolved by partnership and agreement, or by domination. Perhaps one would emerge as the leader over the other. Still, even this kind of discourse wouldn't become the basis for what we understand as human rights.

Our two must become at least three, and realistically a fair many more, before we see those with less power making claims based on something more than a transactional contract with the others. They rely on a developing idea of society and the collective, as well as the individual interests of everyone in it.

There are competing theories about where human rights come from and why. Crucially, we will see how their development is completely intertwined with every complex episode in the history of human society. Attempts at uncoupling them are always a mistake.

I write as a practical lawyer and campaigner of thirty years; not as a philosopher or historian. As a legislator, I make distinctions between laws and policies with which I disagree and those which seem clearly to violate dignity and human rights. Denying the vote or adult minimum wage to seventeen-year-olds sits in the first category, but not to allow these guarantees to some of them on the basis of their sex or race would fall into the second.

There must be clarity, as without it, rights defenders are vulnerable to accusations of anti-democratic tendencies, or, worse still, to charges of cherry-picking; even of modifying rights for their own political convenience. Human rights must be defended against complaints that they are individualistic and selfish rather than uniting; that they are ethnocentric and western rather than universal.

In a healthy political community, comfortable in its skin, and which debates the application of human rights in policy and lawmaking, judges need not become overly politicized.

Nor need human rights invade, rather than inform, the business of elected governments that respect the rule of law.

I will consider various baskets of human rights and the positive and negative obligations on the state to actively deliver them or not to interfere. Civil and political liberties are essential to democratic life; as are social, economic and cultural rights to any quality of existence. Very few rights are described as 'absolute' but many are 'qualified', or limited by protections for other people. What can they help us decide? What are their necessary limits? These questions are essential if rights are not to be distorted and devalued beyond recognition. How much can we 'proportionately interfere' with qualified rights, say, to privacy, speech, protest or property? Where are the potential clashes between them?

The often neglected principle of equal treatment is essential to understanding and delivering human rights. As wars and pandemics – which bring death and hardship to some and eye-watering windfalls to others – so graphically demonstrate, human rights must to some extent seek to address the asymmetry of both power and protection that lies at the heart of every major injustice. However, they cannot by themselves resolve them.

Human rights evolved from the ethical, moral and political frameworks of individuals and communities through struggle. They now inform those frameworks in return. Their sparse but often lyrical drafting conceals tales of court-room drama, political imprisonment, persecution, death, torture and fighting the evil fiction of racial supremacy in the air, on land and on the high seas.

If you read the texts quietly, you can almost hear distant drums and liberation songs. Still, they also provide some binding obligations that must be enforceable in law against states, and perhaps even supra-national public and private bodies in the near future. Ethics, morals, politics and law often overlap, but not so much as to undermine the importance of their distinctions.

The late great legal philosopher Ronald Dworkin described these clearly and compellingly. Ethics inform my personal choices; morals, how I relate to others. Politics is the way that communities and societies make decisions; and laws, one important way of declaring and enforcing these choices.

As in Eleanor Roosevelt's famous adage that human rights begin 'in small places, close to home',[2] it is in the personal sphere that we first apply our values and experience our rights and freedoms.

A parent attempts to raise their child with age-appropriate levels of agency and protection. They seek to monitor, vet and limit the child's access to outside influences in both the real and virtual worlds. Whether consciously or not, these decisions involve ethical and moral questions of the young person's right to privacy, expression and association, and appropriate limits on these things. The political community, as ultimately represented by its lawmakers, grapples with similar questions on behalf of all children.

While most modern democracies will grant a considerable latitude to individual parents to make informed decisions in the interests of their children, they will also set some enforceable legal parameters. Indeed, not to do so would be a violation of the rights of the child. When these rules are breached there will be a range of both civil and criminal legal consequences for those responsible (whether drug dealers, pornographers, social media platforms, educators, or the parents themselves).

However, the ultimate legal, as opposed to ethical or moral, *human rights* obligation to provide both respect and protection of the child will rest with the state. A parent may be cruel or neglectful and legally accountable for this under the ordinary laws of the land, namely criminal and child protection law. Still, what is commonly understood to be the 'human rights violation' is when the state does not adequately protect its children.

Human rights do not replace private ethical and moral choices, nor public, political and policy decisions with legal ones. Instead, they should inform all of these. When a child protection regime is challenged, perhaps for setting a minimum age for alcohol consumption or social media access that is deemed either too low or too high, the courts can be expected to give considerable respect ('deference' in domestic courts and a 'margin of appreciation' in international ones) to the democratic authority and deliberations of those who designed the scheme.

However, courts are nonetheless essential referees. This may be little more than a modern evolution of the rule of law that has long bound governments and the governed. While democracy and human rights are distinct creatures, they must walk hand in hand. As human progress has required larger and more complex public and private institutions, so it correspondingly requires that these be held to account via both the popular vote and the law.

Outside the home, a self-styled 'whistleblower' or a 'freedom fighter' considers how to respond to the abusive behaviour of a corporation or government. In extreme circumstances they may decide to breach civil or criminal law, perhaps by revealing trade or state secrets or by taking even more dramatic direct action. Even if you share my view that such conduct might be justified in the face of tyranny, the decision to break the law is just the beginning of this person's ethical maze.

Human rights provide a significant guide even to what kind

of illegal conduct may be conscionable. I am talking here about human rights values and principles rather than laws, for two reasons. Firstly, human rights and other constitutional laws, like broad duties to respect privacy, rarely apply directly to individuals but instead to state agencies. Secondly, the subject of our hypothetical dilemma has already decided to break the law.

They may have broken duties of confidence to their employer, official secrets legislation or laws against breaking and entering, in pursuit of their view of the greater public interest in exposing grave abuses of power. Yet human rights principles, like the duty to demonstrate 'proportionality' and be no more intrusive than necessary, which usually serve to limit police power, must now act as moral constraint on our self-appointed ethical hero.

The whistleblowing journalist should redact the names of innocents who might otherwise be put in harm's way. The freedom fighter who attacks the dictator's arsenal should avoid harming people (as opposed to property) in general, and civilians in particular. By 'taking the law into their own hands', the outlaw, however well intentioned, has taken on a far greater moral obligation to consider the human rights consequences of their actions. They have perhaps acquired even a level of obligation normally reserved for those who act on behalf of the state. In a further twist, this may in turn become a solid legal consideration for any court subsequently deciding how to deal with this law-breaking 'in the public interest'.

In the face of present global challenges – health and wealth inequality, technological revolution, violent conflict and climate emergency – our human rights will be tested. Rights thinking does not provide perfect solutions to these acute problems, but it can be of assistance and enduring value in addressing them.

Critics deploy a number of familiar, if contradictory, straw men. They complain that elite lawyers and judges use human rights law to try to trump politics and democracy. Yet these rights critics often fail to consider that ground rules and referees are essential to democracy itself.

They lament the many violations that are not prevented as opposed to being challenged under rights laws after the fact, and the latitude that judges grant to governments (the opposite of the 'trumping democracy' criticism). They paint human rights as the enemy of either liberty or security, and deliberately ignore the presence of both of these values within its carefully calibrated scheme of protection.

Some point to noisy human rights pushback in the face of political authoritarianism, as if the former were somehow responsible for the latter, rather than the other way round. Some of these arguments are like suggesting that the legal prohibition of murder fails to prevent it being committed in the first place, and even leads to significant numbers of unresolved crimes.

Disturbingly, they attack both the foundational and universalist claims of human rights as greater threats to citizenship and the nation state than international crime, pandemics, global corporations or climate change. These arguments and the ideologies behind them are far from new. A certain kind of nationalism and its close cousin imperialism have always preferred that rights be restricted to 'citizens', 'free men' or some other necessarily exclusionary category of humanity.

It goes without saying that when the Barons extracted Magna Carta from King John at Runnymede in 1215, they very clearly did not have the rights of serfs, women or foreigners in mind. Despite or perhaps because of these imperfections of the past, there are English sentimentalists who will claim the

Great Charter as their own while berating international human rights. Their US and French counterparts do the same around the Declaration of Independence in 1776 and the Declaration of the Rights of Man and of the Citizen in 1789, respectively.

If these 'rights nationalists' are sceptical of or even hostile to the development of international human rights, they argue that there was a historical 'break' before the Universal Declaration of Human Rights in 1948 (or even before the rights revolutions of the late 1960s). This alleged fracture is supposedly so clean and dramatic that other accounts (Lynn Hunt's being an excellent example) of universal rights being rooted in or at least inspired by much earlier stories and struggles must be pure fiction.

I disagree. Magna Carta is of course a primitive instrument which discriminates against those who were excluded from full personhood in its time. Clause 54 provides that 'No one shall be arrested or imprisoned on the appeal of a woman for the death of any person except her husband' (thereby allowing her to give lawful witness to her husband's murder but no one else's – not even her child's). The clause highlights gross legal and institutional inequality. Nonetheless, the more famous and inspirational clause 39 – 'No free man shall be seized or imprisoned . . . except by the lawful judgement of his equals or by the law of the land' – began the human rights journey to the 'fair trial' or 'due process' that continues to this day.

Enlightenment is not a single age but a continuous process. The evolution of human imagination and empathy (greatly enhanced by literacy, culture, travel and other forms of communication, as well as by knowledge and understanding of our darker histories of tyranny) inevitably broadened our notions of personhood, citizenship and rights. To recognize the rights of foreign nationals and children today is no more or less alien than it once seemed to respect those of women, people of other races or in bondage.

Post-war liberation movements were infused with human rights yearnings as well as with republican nationalism. The Universal Declaration of Human Rights in 1948, the European Convention on Human Rights in 1950 and the Refugee Convention in 1951 are no less rooted in earlier struggles against punishment without trial and slavery for being international. Of course, those documents had to cross borders in an age of aeroplanes, atomic weapons and aspirations for a modicum of global governance.

It should be even more obvious now in the twenty-first century, with its billionaire-owned global corporations, that neither history nor oppression ends with nation states. There can be no self-determination of the people without some self-determination of the person. When power is so concentrated and supra-national, so must be at least some of the means of holding power to account.

Yet while nationalists happily champion the more exclusionary rights of citizenship (afforded by and for a political community on the basis of its various chosen thresholds: nationality, age, sex, residence, language or property), human rights at home and abroad are an obvious threat to a world view that stops at the checkpoint. The chauvinist who rails against the influence of international ideas – including jurisprudence – is not so unlike the one who detests foreign food or the one who resents the reach of law into his home to protect his wife or his child – especially from him.

This exclusionary thinking is simply insufficient in our modern world. If internationalism offers global travel, trade and terrorism, it must also stand for the recognition and protection of all people and their basic rights. How can we hope to take on the contemporary challenges of global inequality, conflict, climate catastrophe and the new and under-governed continent of the internet, without shared values, higher laws and some reasonably credible way of enforcing them?

In the latter part of this book, I discuss what the practical realization of protection might look like in the second half of the twenty-first century. We must make our most agreed-upon fundamental freedoms accessible, both in the popular understanding and in actual redress (rather than being idealized and illusory), in every part of human society.

For too many people, human rights reside in the sanctity of the court room, with lawyers and judges as the priesthood. For a great many others, the ultimate court is that of public opinion with politicians and commentators as oracles. For my part, I believe that human rights values must animate living rooms, class rooms and court rooms; cabinet, interrogation and even war rooms.

While everyone is welcome, this book is not principally for lawyers. It is a reflection on human rights for people across the democratic spectrum, whether instinctive supporters or sceptics. I seek to resist or where necessary translate technical language and to equip you, the reader, with the tools for further investigation and constructive debate.

All human disputes are ultimately resolved by violence, negotiation, politics, adjudication, or some combination of the above. Rights and freedoms, while they are a celebration of the individual, are supposed to help communities navigate conflict without constant or regular recourse to war. It is easy to look at our world and see that human rights are 'not winning' in this important respect.

We should all feel ownership of our hard-won rights and freedoms. How else can we grow in confidence in all the arguments about how they should be applied? To lack a general memory or understanding of what our most basic rights are is to walk even more vulnerably in the world. It is to be robbed of a human heritage as important as numeracy, literacy, art, science, sport and music.

The nurse, the coder and the actor should be able to argue about whether the judge or the politician got a particular decision just about right or completely wrong. That is what a truly free society looks like. When we all feel more empowered, this framework of precious protections will be less open to attack by vested interests in populist clothing. It will be ever-more potent in protecting people and planet for generations to come.

1.
Foundations

The function of freedom is to free somebody else.

Toni Morrison[1]

All history is contested and the relatively young project of human rights history is as fiercely debated as any other. This is hardly surprising when in so many parts of the world the survival of human rights themselves hangs in the balance. It is always tempting to look to the past both for explanations of the present and prescriptions for the future. We are taught to remember history so as not to be forced to repeat it.[2] Some scholars of human rights history reach for the broadest and most heroic roots, while others make umpteen national, historical and conceptual distinctions between various struggles, either presenting human rights as a late twentieth-century confection, unsuitable for uncritical adoption, or conversely pointing out the danger of taking meaningful universal acceptance and inevitability for granted.[3]

We can learn from each of these camps. On the one hand, human struggles for survival, personhood and justice have the deepest roots. On the other, there are any number of distinctions to be made between campaigns within a nation state towards citizenship, and demands for either a lot less, or a great deal more than political inclusion and empowerment. The language of human rights may be employed both by grassroots movements seeking greater equality and by powerful elites defending property and status. In all cases, there may be other, or at least mixed, motives in mind, not least when human rights violations are offered as an argument for war.

The justifications for fundamental rights and freedoms easily fall into two categories. In the first are versions and adaptations of 'natural law' and 'human dignity' where human rights come ultimately from God, from the primacy of human beings on our planet, or some other fundamental case that, if not scientifically provable, has been readily adopted by millions. If human beings are special, for having been created in a maker's image or acquiring special attributes and responsibilities over each other and the world, we must also attract equivalent protections that cannot be overridden by the mere laws of men, however popular or powerful. Critics say this way of thinking is outmoded, ethnocentric, or too easy for all sides in any rights dispute to assert in their own favour.

The alternative arguments for human rights are more utilitarian. Political communities require ground rules. Without basic protections from, for example, arbitrary detention or for freedom of association and speech, the resulting turmoil would lead to the persecution of minority opinion or identities and provoke perpetual violence. It is certainly hard to conceive of how anything approaching an approximation of democracy could survive for more than a very short time without such foundations.

However, all other 'ordinary' laws, such as those prohibiting criminal and civil wrongs, protecting property, the family and so on, are in no small part also aimed at conflict avoidance and the good society. Further, human rights include social, economic and cultural freedoms as well as civil and political ones. They protect children, refugees, prisoners and others excluded from political life as well as full citizens. Therefore the higher ethics and laws of human rights transcend this reasoning too.

It is no coincidence that justifications for rights often mirror the political authority of the time. When monarchs ruled by divine right and there were only embryonic democratic developments, the claim for the rights of man needed a similarly divine source. As societies reformed around communitarian legitimacy towards greater democracy, so rights thinking similarly evolved.

As a result, it is a blend of spiritual, ethical and practical justifications that has illuminated so many minds for so long. This classic cocktail with varying amounts of each ingredient for personal taste comes closest to explaining why we have had to promote human rights ever since we began to live together in increasingly complex societies.

For my part, I believe human rights celebrate and protect everything that humans need in order to survive and thrive in this world. They are our best attempt at respecting human dignity. It is against this yardstick that we must measure their content, limitations, application, clashes and enforcement. There are no effective human rights without a good society to protect them. Without respect for fundamental rights and freedoms, no good society will endure.

Definitions

So that I can better explain the argument to follow, I hope you will forgive me setting out *what I mean* by a number of everyday words that are often used rather more loosely. Precision is important in the face of human rights opponents armed with both the needle and the sledgehammer.

Ethics are a system of personal judgements about how I behave and the **principles** that guide me in these decisions. People often talk about professional and other group ethics, but these are a lot closer to **law** when they are translated into rules that a group enforces against its members, or that the state enforces against that group.

Morals overlap with ethics – and the terms are often used interchangeably. But morals immediately suggest judgements, principles and tests of wider shared ownership and application. Morals can get a bad rap thanks to centuries of patriarchy and overly censorious religion. But they nonetheless represent an indispensable web of non-legal, yet vital ethical **obligations**, duties or responsibilities. People in families and other communities, local and global, feel that they owe these duties to each other, even when no one is looking and there is no recourse to law.

Politics is the way in which societies organize themselves and represent different views about how they should be run. It includes rival theories of everything from the economy to international relations, as well as the business of actually legislating for and administering communities, countries, continents and the world. Economics is a key branch of politics, though some prefer to mystify it, putting highly contentious theories beyond debate in maintenance of the status quo. I do not accept that politics or economics are anything like natural science. Science pursues an explanation of what *is*. Politics argues for different versions of what *ought to be*. Attempts to suggest comparisons between natural science and 'political science' deny that the world can be organized in any number of ways. They disempower millions of ordinary people in their democratic political agency.

Law is a system of enforceable rights and obligations. Some law originates in the assemblies, parliaments and other legislatures of nations, some in the agreements that people and even nations strike with each other, and some in the binding decisions of judges who interpret laws and deal with the gaps within them when people come in need of impartial resolution of their disputes.

Justice has perhaps become too grand, broad and subjective a term to grapple with fully here. Used narrowly, it can refer to the legal and court system of any land or community and their theories of dispute resolution. Yet it is too often a euphemism for fairness in the broadest sense. People articulate their personal theories of social, economic, gender and racial 'justice' sometimes as a way to avoid talking about specific disputes in overtly political or controversial terms. I shall seek to avoid this elephant trap by using the term 'justice' sparingly.

Values are broad ideas, some are even instinctual – often shared and as often contested, at least in application – as to how we should live our best lives. I put intimate concepts of love, kindness, self and mutual respect, as well as more political ones of liberty, equality, competition and solidarity in this category. Our values inform our ethics, morals, politics and law, even though we as individuals and societies do not always practise what we preach. Values necessarily inform human rights, both in their formulation (as when treaties, constitutions and human rights laws are drafted) and in practice, in the hands of officials, politicians, lawyers and judges who interpret them. The most important value underpinning contemporary human rights is that of **dignity**.

Dignity is very often written about as the philosophical basis for fundamental human rights. Still, Ronald Dworkin's work takes some beating.[4] He wrote about the twin test of treating all people as being of equal worth and respecting their individual agency. This brings harmony to the apparently competing ideals of liberty and equality which underpin all the international norms and domestic constitutional human rights (for example, against torture, slavery, discrimination and for access to justice, privacy, free speech, voting, shelter, healthcare, education etc.) that are worth having. Dworkin was right to say that the value contained in liberty is something quite different from unfettered freedom. One does not have to engage in mental gymnastics to justify the prohibition of murder, and to ban it does not interfere with a person's liberty. I have long thought that those who believe that liberty and equality are in permanent and inevitable conflict should imagine asking an enslaved person which of the two they crave.

Rights are mirrors of obligations. They suggest a claim to which I am entitled. People speak of moral rights in all sorts of contexts, but *legal* rights are supposed to grant me a means of enforcing the duty that I am owed. *Civil* rights are the civil and political rights and freedoms that I seek to achieve and enforce in my political community. *Constitutional* rights are those that are given an even higher legal status by a political community (like, for example, making it harder for the government and legislature of the moment to change them).

Human rights have a place within each of these concepts. They are represented in the international and domestic laws of global, continental and national political communities, and in many instances create legally enforceable rights and obligations. Yet they also spring from and speak to our most basic values, informing our personal ethics, community morals, national and international politics.

They are reflected in many of the other laws that do not come with any obvious human rights symbolism or carry its tag. The right to life is partly protected by the criminal offence of murder, and the rule against torture is embedded within grave crimes of violence and rape. Protection from slavery may be pursued by laws against false imprisonment, and for a minimum wage.

Detailed criminal procedure and mental health laws have been tested and improved by rights against arbitrary detention and to fair trials. Rights to respect for private and family life have required limits upon police powers, and to the disproportionate separation of family members via immigration and divorce law. A host of civil and criminal laws protect our property rights. Electoral laws should guarantee our enfranchisement.

Crucially, human rights belong to all human beings just by virtue of being alive. They continue to 'exist' even in places where they are constantly violated or not officially recognized. They can neither be given nor taken away by the political community. This book is about **why** this must be, and **how** it will be of continuing benefit to humanity long after my generation have had our shot at writing what the good Professor Dworkin called a 'subscript to our mortality'.[5] We can make our lives tiny diamonds in the cosmic sands or leave only coal dust behind.

Some History

Tom Bingham (Lord Bingham of Cornhill, KG, PC, FBA) was perhaps the greatest judge of what we call the common law world, where judges are especially important in developing the law by a system of binding precedents, applying principles to factual circumstances. During the turbulent first decade of the twenty-first century, he was a towering figure, serving as the United Kingdom's Senior Law Lord, before the advent of the Supreme Court, an institution that was his vision. A student of history before he came to the law, he began his now modern classic *The Rule of Law*[6] with a little history to help put subsequent explanation in context. Some of these moments are also vital to the birth and development of human rights.

As the rule of law is only the foundation upon which human rights and democracy are necessarily built, my history must be a little broader. Nonetheless, like Bingham's, my selections are limited and will reflect where and how on the planet I have lived and worked. There are already many large volumes devoted to human rights history, and there are many more still to be written across the continents and from different perspectives. I share these fragments only to help explain my thinking.

The Cyrus Cylinder (539 BCE)

This clay cylinder is named after the king of the ancient Persian Empire. After conquering Babylon, he unusually freed the slaves and declared freedom of religion and equality among races. Scholars argue about the extent to which the cylinder records these rights in the Akkadian language. However, they are now reflected in the first four Articles of the Universal Declaration of Human Rights, providing that all humans are born free and equal, that they have the right to be free of discrimination, that they have the right to life and liberty and to be free from slavery. The cylinder script has been translated into each of the six official languages of the United Nations.

Aristotle (384–322 BCE)

This ancient Greek philosopher argued for the existence of a natural moral order. He made a vital distinction between 'natural' and 'legal' justice:

> the natural is that which has the same validity everywhere and does not depend upon acceptance.[7]

Aristotle's natural justice is inherent and universal regardless of whether it has been embraced by a particular political community. This is essentially what we say about 'inalienable' rights and freedoms in the world today. The rule against torture, for example, is considered so fundamental that it binds all governments as a principle of international law, regardless of whether they are even signatories to the relevant UN Convention. Signatories undertake to provide 'legal justice' and prosecute or extradite torturers regardless of their nationality or the place where they perpetrated their crimes.

Ashoka (c. 304–232 BCE)

Also commonly known as Ashoka the Great, he ruled most of the Indian subcontinent for around thirty-five years. After conquering the state of Kalinga in around 260 BCE, he is thought to have been particularly troubled by the mass casualties and so converted to Buddhism, which he then spent much of the rest of his life promoting. He promised never again to wage a war of conquest and issued edicts which were inscribed upon publicly visible pillars and walls in parts of his Mauryan Empire – modern-day Afghanistan, Bangladesh, India, Nepal and Pakistan. They were arguably rather ahead of their time, being mostly moral and political rather than religious in nature, referring to matters such as benevolent government and uniform judicial process.

Thomas Aquinas (1225–1274)

This Italian priest and philosopher wrote many commentaries on Aristotle's work and promoted the theory of 'natural law'. It was one of his four categories of law, alongside the eternal, human and divine. He is largely responsible for medieval Christian interest in Aristotle's work. He wrote of natural law:

> this is the first precept of the law, that good is to be done and pursued, and evil is to be avoided. All other precepts of the natural law are based on this.[8]

Magna Carta (1215)

This famous document is no doubt far more cited than read. But it still has a vital place in the development of both the rule of law and human rights laws. Much has been written about Magna Carta's modest virtues and extreme limitations. It was written in Latin (thus inaccessible to most of the population), extracted from King John under duress from the Barons, and accordingly annulled by the Pope within months. It is, inevitably, hugely discriminatory to modern eyes. Still, the document employed language from earlier royal charters and even the coronation oath to grant rights to all free men in the land. The cultural and mythical significance of Magna Carta as a symbol for holding power to account is perhaps just as important as its actual content. Nonetheless, Bingham rightly described the following extracts as having 'the power to make the blood race':[9]

39. No free man shall be seized or imprisoned or stripped of his rights or possessions, or outlawed or exiled, or deprived of his standing in any other way, nor will we proceed with force against him, or send others to do so, except by the lawful judgment of his equals or by the law of the land.

40. To no one will we sell, to no one deny or delay right or justice.

Habeas corpus ad subjiciendum (from 1305)

The legendary English jurist and Conservative politician William Blackstone chronicled the first use of this 'writ', or order, requiring that a person's detention be accounted for in court in 1305. However, similar procedural writs were probably used even earlier. Bingham wrote that:

> In *Bushell's Case*,[10] decided in 1670, Chief Justice Vaughan was able to assert as simple fact: 'The writ of habeas corpus is now the most usual remedy by which a man is restored to his liberty, if he have been against law deprived of it.' The simplicity of the writ is its strength and its virtue. It has been widely recognized as the most effective remedy against executive lawlessness that the world has ever seen, a remedy introduced and developed by the judges and adopted elsewhere, notably in the United States.[11]

This procedure is still used to challenge and end unlawful detention all over the common law world. It has also informed the right against arbitrary detention in the Universal Declaration of Human Rights, regional human rights treaties and constitutions and bills of rights all over the planet.

Outlawing torture (from 1215)

The deliberate infliction of severe pain as punishment, or to extract information or confession, is a very old practice that sadly continues in many parts of the world today, despite global condemnation and treaties. Attempts to abolish this particular form of cruelty also go back a very long way. Like the struggle for fair trials, campaigns against torture are one of the longest and most continuous strands in human rights thinking. The two are also intertwined.

Like many other writers on the subject, Bingham gives particular significance to the ruling of the Fourth Lateran Council of Pope Innocent III that 'trial by ordeal' was cruel and therefore not to be blessed. This practice of subjecting a suspect to holding or walking upon hot metal or to drowning was based upon the idea that God would intervene to save an innocent person. As this practice fell out of favour, the English and Welsh authorities and their continental counterparts adopted different procedures for determining guilt. While the common law system did not allow a defendant to testify, witnesses could be called against the witnesses for the accuser. One witness was enough and a jury would simply decide who and what it believed. The continental system was more onerous, requiring at least two corroborating accusing witnesses or a confession. As these were often not available, the authorities resorted to extracting confessions by torture.

It was easy for common law commentators to be almost self-congratulatory about this apparent fork in the road,[12] not least as it drew admiration from anti-torture campaigners such as Voltaire[13] across the English Channel. However, as the eminent American historian Lynn Hunt points out, practices of torture as well as those of inhuman and degrading treatment or punishment and death continued across all the nations of the British Isles, as elsewhere in the world, for a very long time. Torture was employed in Britain into the sixteenth and seventeenth centuries for sedition (by virtue of the Royal Prerogative) and witchcraft.

> Brutal forms of punishment upon conviction were ubiquitous in Europe and the Americas. Although the British Bill of Rights of 1689 expressly prohibited cruel punishment, judges still sentenced criminals to the whipping post, ducking stool, stocks, pillory, branding, and execution by drawing and quartering (dismemberment by horses) or, for women, drawing and quartering and burning at the stake.[14]

Hunt goes on to describe how Britain exported torture to its colonies, a point not lost upon fellow historian Samuel Moyn in his own account of how even in the twentieth and twenty-first centuries, and after an Amnesty International campaign resulted in the UN Convention against Torture in 1985, western democratic powers were prepared to dabble in torture overseas. Notorious examples arose during the Kenyan Mau Mau uprising from 1952, and in Iraq, Guantánamo and so-called black sites to which people were 'rendered' during the War on Terror following 9/11. Nonetheless, Hunt also highlights the international importance of the 1764 pamphlet 'An Essay on Crimes and Punishments' by the Italian Cesare Beccaria. Quickly translated into French and English, it was groundbreaking in rejecting not only torture and cruel punishment, but also the death penalty that so often followed.

> After reading Beccaria, the English jurist William Blackstone made the connection that would become characteristic ever

> after of the Enlightenment view; the criminal law, affirmed Blackstone, should always be 'conformable to the dictates of truth and justice, the feelings of humanity and the indelible rights of mankind.'[15]

Despite many examples of and arguments about torture to this day, we see the beginnings of widespread opposition to it in the human rights language of the 1700s. Moyn warns against torture as a 'taboo', or a means of singling it out for exceptional revulsion, perhaps at the expense of looking at broader cruelty and the systems that perpetuate it.[16]

I understand the dangers of focusing on an extreme cruelty which we believe to be in global decline (notwithstanding the 'War on Terror'). However, to single out rights against torture and slavery as absolute (as the drafters of domestic laws and international human rights treaties have now long done) is simply to point out that they can never be qualified or justified. It is not to flinch from the principle that all human rights – like dignity itself – are indivisible. It is not to argue that other rights are less important.

Why is torture never justified? Because as some understood even in the Middle Ages, in seeking to extract what the torturer wants to hear, the practice is inherently unreliable. It therefore inflicts cruelty upon often innocent people. Even when the extreme cruelty is directed towards the guilty, including those who would do such things to others, it invites cruelty in return and damages the dignity and humanity of victim, perpetrator and the wider society looking on.

Whatever our views on eating meat, a great many of those who have historically reared and killed animals for human consumption still consider themselves to be animal lovers. Death, it is argued, even for creatures bred or hunted for the benefit of humans, need not of itself be cruel. Despite heated debates about the precise parameters of cruelty to animals as opposed to humans, most societies believe even animal cruelty to be fundamentally wrong. 'Inhuman' as opposed to 'humane' behaviour describes the perpetrator not the victim.

So the human right against torture is absolute, while the right to life is qualified by exceptions in war and self-defence. I wrote my justification for this distinction in 2014, after well over a decade of discussion with human rights lawyers, campaigners and a variety of challenging public audiences:

> We don't all like to talk about it, but we will all die one day. In practical terms an absolute 'right to life' would require medical miracles rather than philosophical or legal development. We can hope for long, happy and fulfilled lives but death will come. Torture and degradation need not. To take another's life and choose the moment of their ending is quite literally to 'play God'. It is, rightly, almost always unacceptable. However, to inflict inhuman treatment is to play a yet more terrifying role, and in so doing to force a fellow human being to endure a darkness of which we should aspire to rid the world.[17]

Hugo Grotius (1583–1645)

Grotius was a Dutch Calvinist jurist, perhaps most often remembered for his writing on the international law of war and of the sea. He was also an important proponent of universal rights and in his work we can see the inevitable logical connections between higher laws between and within nations. He wrote about their source being the Creator, or human nature, or perhaps both, if the latter were designed by the former:

> The law of nature is a dictate of right reason, which points out that an act, according as it is or is not in conformity with rational nature, has in it a quality of moral baseness or moral necessity; and that in consequence, such an act is either forbidden or enjoined.[18]

Revolutionary American and French Declarations and Rights (1776 and 1789)

It is perhaps an oversimplification to observe that revolution in America preceded that in France, but that the French agreed their constitutional 'rights of man and the citizen' just before their allies in the new United States of America agreed the Bill of Rights. More importantly, there was a great deal of international collaboration and cross-fertilization in these revolutionary and rights projects, as exemplified by the activist travels and writing of the English-born philosopher Thomas Paine[19] among many others. Further, even while preceding both the French Declaration of the Rights of Man and the Citizen and the US Bill of Rights by over thirteen years, the US Declaration of Independence is itself heavily laced in human rights language:

> We hold these truths to be self-evident, that all men are created equal, that they are endowed by their Creator with certain unalienable Rights, that among these are Life, Liberty and the pursuit of Happiness. That to secure these rights, Governments are instituted among Men, deriving their just powers from the consents of the governed. That whenever any Form of Government becomes destructive of these ends, it is the Right of the People to alter or to abolish it, and to institute new Government, laying its foundations on such principles and

> organizing its powers in such form, as to them shall seem most likely to effect their Safety and Happiness.

These words, principally drafted by Thomas Jefferson and adopted in Congress in 1776, are astonishingly clear in a number of respects. All 'men' are equal; not only the citizens of any one nation, state or federation. There are some 'unalienable' rights that come not from government, nor even from consent, but from the 'Creator'. Indeed, it is the 'Right of the People to alter or to abolish' governments that, instead of securing these rights, become destructive to them. It created no rights that could be enforceable in a court of law. They would come later. However, there can be little doubt that the Declaration intended to argue for a law that is higher than any that can be instituted by a single political community. After all, it had to justify breaking away from the community that was the British Empire, once it had become 'necessary for one people to dissolve the political bands which have connected them with another'.[20]

Jefferson was a friend of the French revolutionary Marquis de Lafayette who was in turn a veteran of the War of American Independence. Jefferson was in Paris in 1789 when Lafayette began drafting a French declaration of rights, months before the fall of the Bastille in July. However, Hunt observes much less sole authorship of the seventeen articles adopted 'by an unwieldy committee of forty deputies', after much detailed and some unresolved disagreement on 27 August.

> The document so frantically cobbled together was stunning in its sweep and simplicity. Never once mentioning king, nobility, or church, it declared the 'natural, inalienable and sacred rights of man' to be the foundation of any and all government . . . More striking than any particular guarantee, however, was the

> universality of the claims made. References to 'men,' 'man,' 'every man,' 'all men,' 'all citizens,' 'each citizen,' 'society,' and 'every society' dwarfed the single reference to the French people.[21]

It protected 'liberty, property, safety and resistance against oppression', unpacking liberty as 'anything that does not harm others'. It guaranteed equal treatment between citizens and the right to contribute to lawmaking 'personally or through their representatives'. It prohibited arbitrary detention and retrospective and disproportionate penalties, and asserted the presumption of innocence. It protected freedom of conscience and religion and of expression, the right to property and information about the necessary and lawful tax regime.

The first ten amendments to the US Constitution that came to be known as the Bill of Rights were approved by Congress in September 1789 and ratified in December 1791. This time James Madison was the principal draftsman. He studied the criticisms of the US Constitution from anti-federalists concerned about federal government riding roughshod over individuals and the states, and of the presidency becoming a monarchy. It was informed by the earlier Virginia Declaration of Rights (1776), Northwest Ordinance (1787), English Bill of Rights (1689) and Magna Carta, as well as the French Declaration.

It guarantees freedom of religion (not least by preventing Congress from establishing one religion over others), free speech, freedom of the press and peaceful assembly. More controversially to some modern eyes, it protects the right to 'bear arms' – though this has at certain times been argued to be merely a right against federal rather than local state government and to be limited to protecting a well-regulated militia.[22] Importantly, the Fourth Amendment protects the right of people 'to be secure in their persons, houses, papers and effects, against unreasonable searches and seizures' and requires that search and seizure warrants shall require 'probable cause' or good reason, argued under oath or affirmation; for example, by a police officer.

Amendments 5 to 8 set out fair trial or due process rights and protection from excessive bail requirements, fines and cruel and unusual punishment. There is the right to indictment – or formal charge – by a Grand Jury in capital and other very serious criminal cases. There is protection from double jeopardy (repeat prosecution for the same offence) and against self-incrimination – being forced to give testimony against oneself. The latter gave rise to the famous case of *Miranda v Arizona* (1966), requiring, as seen in a thousand Hollywood movies, that suspects be informed of their rights to a lawyer and against self-incrimination before police interrogation. There is a right to speedy and public jury trial, for a defendant to be informed of the case against them, and to be allowed to confront prosecution witnesses. Defendants have a right to a process for compelling witnesses in their favour and to legal assistance.

These criminal procedural protections have long been seen as a gold standard. They influenced much later international human rights treaties and national constitutions and laws, even in countries without jury trial.

Still, we shouldn't be too starry-eyed about either the original United States or French constitutional rights settlements. While groundbreaking, they were also of their time. Hunt reminds us that Jefferson was 'a slaveowner, and Lafayette, an aristocrat'. More importantly perhaps, despite poetic, universalist and egalitarian language, both regimes excluded women, children, foreigners, prisoners, people without property and other categories of humanity from anything approaching meaningful rights protection. Notably, the first French Declaration did not prevent the revolutionary massacres and public executions of 'the Terror' to come, nor did the first version of the US Bill of Rights end slavery.

Slave trade abolition (1772–1888)

Slavery, like torture which has played such a large part in it, is an ancient evil. Like the campaigns against torture, those against slavery took on an international dimension long before the post-World War II era of comprehensive rights treaties. This was necessarily the case with the infamous transatlantic slave trade – which began in the 1400s and peaked in the 1780s – as so many different empires, nations and territories were involved.

American jurist and Provost of Stanford University Professor Jenny Martinez begins her book *The Slave Trade and the Origins of International Human Rights Law*[23] with the epic tale of Samuel Adjai Crowther and Henry Leeke. The former was kidnapped at the age of thirteen from a part of West Africa that is now Nigeria and trafficked into slavery. After being liberated, he went on to become the first African bishop in the Anglican Church. The latter was the British Royal Navy Captain who in 1822 was empowered by international law to intercept the ship that transported Crowther:

> In Freetown sat a new international tribunal established to enforce the treaties prohibiting the slave trade. Most people think of international courts as an innovation of the twentieth century, with the Nuremberg trials of the Nazi war criminals at the end of World War II being the first real effort to use international law to prosecute those accused of gross human rights abuses. But more than a century before

> Nuremberg, international courts in Sierra Leone, Cuba, Brazil and other places across the Atlantic heard cases related to the slave trade, the original 'crime against humanity.'[24]

In a simultaneously scholarly and enthralling work, Martinez goes on to explain how the legal system that was first used to legitimize the slave trade came to outlaw it, in nation states, upon the high seas and globally. Equally, she explains how it was that the British Empire that had been so unjustly enriched from the evil trade in millions of human beings came not only to turn away from it, but would prove instrumental in its wider decline. It did this via a combination of the unilateral exercise of pre-eminent nineteenth-century naval strength, bribery, negotiation and law.

Motives were no doubt mixed. Once domestic public opinion, the courts and Parliament had turned against slavery, British commercial interests sought to remove any unfair advantage to rival plantation owners and trading nations. However, the transatlantic abolition movement, increasingly fuelled by the eloquent testimony of liberated survivors, spoke human rights language with a natural law accent.

While much earlier proponents of natural law had made exceptions and excuses for slavery – some of them not unlike modern-day excuses for treating foreign nationals very differently from our own – by the late eighteenth and early nineteenth century, these were wearing thin in politically influential Enlightenment and religious circles. Grotius had once justified slavery as collateral to war,[25] saying that it created an incentive for conquering armies to keep prisoners alive. Even John Locke,[26] in the seventeenth century, believed that slavery might be an acceptable alternative in situations where a man might justly be killed. A century later, the French philosopher Jean-Jacques Rousseau[27] took an absolute position against slavery, and towards the end of the eighteenth century, some were beginning to argue that slavery was contrary to English law.[28] Yet the slave trade was still permitted by the laws of nations. The stage was set for a dramatic clash between domestic law and international law, and between the rights of man and laws of men.

The 1772 landmark case of *Somerset v Stewart*[29] is perhaps better known internationally than in England where Lord Mansfield decided it. James Somerset had been brought to England from America by his 'master' Charles Stewart in 1769. Two years later Somerset escaped and, upon his recapture, was imprisoned on a ship bound for the then British colony of Jamaica, with instructions from Stewart that he be sold to a plantation owner. English abolitionists (both black and white) helped Somerset file for *habeas corpus* to seek his release. Their lawyers argued that slavery was contrary to both natural law and the common law of England, there being no parliamentary statute authorizing it. Stewart's team argued the primacy of property and that the rule on 'conflicts of laws' meant that Virginia slave ownership should be respected in England. They warned of a 'floodgates' effect that would otherwise liberate thousands of slaves worth hundreds of thousands of pounds to their 'owners'. Mansfield found:

> The state of slavery is of such a nature that it is incapable of being introduced on any reasons, moral or political but only positive law, which preserves its force long after the reasons, occasion, and time itself from whence it was created, is erased from memory. It is so odious, that nothing can be suffered to support it, but positive law.

Crucially, an English court did this five years before the State of Vermont became the first post-revolutionary American republic to abolish slavery in 1777, and thirty-five years before the British Parliament passed the Abolition of the Slave Trade Act in 1807. France would not effectively abolish slavery until 1848. US President Abraham Lincoln would proclaim the emancipation of slaves in 1862 to have effect the following January. Still, the Thirteenth Amendment to the Constitution – banning slavery – would not follow until 1865. That was ninety-three years after the Somerset case.

Perhaps unsurprisingly, the anti-slave trade chapter is underwritten in human rights history. Proponents of human rights after World War II included leaders of victorious powers, who had good reason to focus on the atrocities of the German Third Reich and Japanese Empire. The older sins of their own nations were inevitably embarrassing in the context of sensitive negotiations with the Soviet Union and in a world where historic western crimes against African peoples were cited by liberation struggles, both on that continent and within the United States. Further, politicians in both pro- and anti-human rights camps burnish their own angelic credentials over rushing to acknowledge the occasions when lawyers and judges were more in tune with public opinion, or earlier to the cause of human dignity. Of this phenomenon, the slave trade would not be the last example.

Peoples' suffrage and women's rights (1718 onwards)

The right to vote is the most classic example of a *civil* right, without which a person cannot be a full member of a democratic political community. Yet those who have been denied it have long employed fundamental human rights, or 'rights of man', arguments for inclusion based upon humanity, personhood and dignity. The works of both Thomas Paine and Mary Wollstonecraft are infused with this kind of language against a more conservative rights narrative that restricted the franchise on the basis of sex, property and religion. Suffrage campaigns and early constitutions, as in France and the Francophone world, were an early stage or rehearsal of arguments for universalism versus particularism around rights. Mary Wollstonecraft's *A Vindication of the Rights of Woman*[30] (1792) is regarded as both the original feminist text and argument for women's education. However, as frailty of the mind was employed as a justification for denying women property and voting rights and used as an explanation of their submission, this advocacy of women's education was inseparable from the wider women's movement that it subsequently inspired:

> Strengthen the female mind by enlarging it, and there will be an end to blind obedience.[31]

In turn, while 'first wave' feminists are strongly associated with legendary campaigns for the vote and political representation, this was very much the 'wedge' issue rather than the only one. Women's suffrage movements at the turn of the nineteenth to the twentieth century learned from earlier anti-slavery struggles and argued for rights to property, education and entry into the professions. They may be described as human rights campaigns, even though some of those involved took a less than universalist or even unsupportive approach to the rights of working-class women and men.[32]

The 1960s and 1970s saw the second wave of the women's movement, with a focus on reproductive rights[33] and women's safety from violence in the home and on the streets, as well as deep-seated social, economic and cultural oppression, rather than merely removing formal legal bars to equality. The wider human rights movement learned much from this thinking, argument and litigation, especially around 'positive obligations' in the face of institutional discrimination.

Discrimination is not simply the unfair differential treatment of people. The sin is often in not intervening to deal with people's different challenges.[34] For example, the employer who does not grant parental leave is harsh to all workers. But the harshness will be worse and have a discriminatory impact on those who bear the children and historically carry more of the childcare burden. A public building may be theoretically open to all, but if there is no ramp or lift in addition to the steep steps (or perhaps just one small step) to its grand entrance, those in wheelchairs are effectively barred. Specific international and domestic laws have been developed to deal with these challenges. They are part of a universal human rights whole.

From world war to universal human rights

It is easy to eulogize the war generation, who overcame enormous privations to defeat the Third Reich and other Axis powers. They combined legendary courage in the face of adversity with ideals and imagination of a different world.[35] It is perhaps also too easy to be cynical about some of the human rights rhetoric used by leaders such as Franklin Roosevelt and Winston Churchill while World War II raged on.

It was no doubt a means of uniting and inspiring often exhausted people, hungry for liberation from deference and from Empire. When President Roosevelt spoke of his Four Freedoms in the State of the Union address in January 1941,

Japan had yet to bomb US naval forces in Pearl Harbor and bring the twentieth-century superpower out of its traditional non-interventionist stance and into the war. Many Americans, like their European cousins, saw the First Great War as an imperialist mistake that they were reluctant to repeat. Neutrality laws placed significant constraint on what could be done to aid the British Empire against Germany, Italy and Japan, even after France had fallen in June 1940. The Soviet Union was in a pact with Germany, only switching sides later, when it was itself invaded by Hitler's forces in June 1941.

The Four Freedoms was a political speech preparing the US for war, not a philosophical text, nor a legal treaty. The freedoms were accordingly light on detail. Nonetheless, the call for a 'world founded on' freedom of speech, of worship, and from want and fear combined two key civil rights (as in the US Constitution) with a growing international consensus around economic development and collective security. The speech provides the germ of what would eventually develop into the United Nations Charter in 1945 and even the Universal Declaration of Human Rights in 1948 – after a great deal of drafting and negotiation.

Churchill had Nazi atrocities more specifically in mind in his now famous letter of October 1942 to William Temple, the Archbishop of Canterbury:

> The systematic cruelties to which the Jewish people – men, women and children – have been exposed under the Nazi regime are amongst the most terrible events of history, and place an indelible stain upon all who perpetrate and instigate them. Free men and women denounce these vile crimes, and when this world struggle ends with the enthronement of human rights, racial persecution will be ended.[36]

Notwithstanding the inevitable double standards of old empires with their at times equivocal or even hostile responses to anti-segregation campaigns at home and liberation struggles abroad, anti-racism was always going to be at the philosophical heart of post-war human rights development. When the full horror of Nazi genocide became evident, this gained momentum. While the UN Charter[37] understandably prioritized world peace, its third line spoke of the need:

> to reaffirm faith in fundamental human rights, in the dignity and worth of the human person, in the equal rights of men and women and of nations large and small . . .

It neither invented human rights, nor did it define them. Development had, in practice, begun long ago, but definition would be left to the work of the Human Rights Commission of the new United Nations during 1947 and 1948. It was chaired by Eleanor Roosevelt, the wife of the wartime US President, and consisted of P. C. Chang of the Republic of China, Charles Malik of Lebanon, William Hodgson of Australia, Hernán Santa Cruz of Chile, René Cassin of France, Alexander Bogomolov of the Soviet Union, Charles Dukes (Baron Dukeston) of the UK and John Humphrey of Canada. Humphrey was a UN official in its new Secretariat and produced the first draft of the list of rights to be included in the Universal Declaration of Human Rights.

However, it is René Cassin who is widely credited for the poetry and structure of the Declaration, including its preamble, general principles and final articles. Cassin was influenced by the Napoleonic Code[38] and compared the Declaration to the portico of a Greek temple. The principles of dignity, liberty, equality and brotherhood served as foundations, the preamble as steps, the main body of the document provided its columns, and the final three articles bound it together as the pediment.

Eleanor Roosevelt's autobiography[39] provides insight into the tensions at play, and into her own inimitable style of attempting to diffuse them with a punishing work ethic and numerous shared cups of tea. The dynamic between Chang, a pluralist citing Confucianist[40] influences, and Malik, the Christian citing Aquinas, was clearly vital in arriving at a universalist text rather than a solely western one. There were also arguments about whether and how to include social and economic rights when the wealth and development disparity between member states was so great. The federal nature of members such as the US and Australia posed a challenge in attributing responsibility for guaranteeing the rights. The Soviets pushed in vain for constant references to 'the State' and bemoaned what they perceived as a preoccupation with old-fashioned civil and political rights.

Perhaps ironically, in the light of later resistance to domestic incorporation and legal enforcement of the human rights covenants that followed, the British delegation was disappointed that the Declaration had no binding legal effect. Tellingly, and notwithstanding the fact that South African Prime Minister Jan Smuts had inserted the concept of dignity into the earlier UN Charter, Charles Te Water, the country's representative under the new National Party government, with its policy of apartheid,[41] fought in vain against the inclusion of dignity in the Declaration that was finally adopted by the UN General Assembly.

Of the fifty-eight members at that time (most current members having achieved sovereignty and membership later on), forty-eight voted in favour and none against. There were eight formal abstentions and Honduras and Yemen failed either to vote or to abstain.

The Saudi Arabian and South African abstentions can be attributed to the inclusion of religious and marriage freedom, and race equality, respectively. The six Soviet Bloc abstentions were formally expressed as a protest against insufficient condemnation of Nazism and fascism in the document. However, they were undoubtedly in no small part a Stalinist response to the inclusion of basic civil liberties, including the rights of citizens to leave from and return to their own countries.

Nonetheless, the scale of the agreement underpinning the foundational document of post-war fundamental human rights is a breathtaking achievement, as yet unrivalled in international statecraft. Its preamble begins:

> Whereas recognition of the inherent dignity and of the equal and inalienable rights of all members of the human family is the foundation of freedom, justice and peace in the world,
>
> Whereas disregard and contempt for human rights have resulted in barbarous acts which have outraged the conscience of mankind, and the advent of a world in which human beings shall enjoy the freedom of speech and belief and freedom from fear and want has been proclaimed as the highest aspiration of the common people,
>
> Whereas it is essential, if man is not to be compelled to have recourse, as a last resort, to rebellion against tyranny and oppression, that human rights should be protected by the law . . .

First came the spark of an idea that even monarchs must be bound by higher, natural and universal laws. It ignited struggles for specific rights to fair trials and against torture and slavery before exploding into the belief in government only by and for the people. Imperialism and nationalism had delivered not one but two terrible global conflicts. The time was surely ripe for constructing a new world order founded on the rule of law and rights of all humanity.

2.

Architecture

Law, say the gardeners, is the sun.

W. H. Auden[1]

A romantic declaration is easier to make than a binding commitment. Even constitutional and international declarations are easier to negotiate than instruments granting enforceable protection. Just as love may be fleeting without duty, human rights need law to give them force.

This was well understood by the drafters of the Universal Declaration, who knew that their enormous achievement was still unenforceable in any courts of law. It would require urgent follow-up in the form of new and binding international legal architecture if its ideals were to be made real. This was especially important in relation to the most vulnerable among us.

Then as now, few were more politically, economically and physically vulnerable than refugees. Remembering the failure of Allied powers to give adequate passage to those desperate to flee the Nazis, even after Kristallnacht in 1938 heralded a policy of systematic genocide, renders refugee protection the most poignant post-war rights paradigm.

The Refugee Convention, 1951

Given the emerging post-war understanding of the sheer horror of preceding years, it is unsurprising that the Refugee Convention should have been one of the earliest priorities of the new international human rights architects. This Convention brought detail and binding effect to supplement the right to asylum in Article 14 of the Universal Declaration. The Refugee Convention came into force in 1954 and has been amended only once by its 1967 protocol. This removed the original limitation of protection to those fleeing European events before 1951. The subsequent protection was intended to be permanent and worldwide.

The Convention defines a refugee as someone with a well-founded fear of persecution, for reasons of race, religion, nationality, membership of a social group or political opinion, who is therefore unable or unwilling to return to their country of origin. It is built upon principles of non-discrimination, non-penalization and *non-refoulement*.

This means the protections should be applied without discrimination on the basis of race, religion or country of origin, but also, as international law has developed over time, on other prohibited grounds such as sex, age, disability, sexuality and so on. It recognizes that the most desperate, genuine refugees may have no choice but to flee – as from the Nazis – via illegal routes using false papers and identities and travel by clandestine means across borders in breach of the ordinary immigration controls of nations. It prohibits penalizing them for, say, crimes relating to their seeking asylum, or arbitrarily detaining them simply for attempting to make a claim. Critically, the Convention prohibits the return or other expulsion of refugees against their will, to places where their lives or freedoms would be in peril. The only narrow exception to this protection is in the case of those who have committed war crimes, crimes against humanity, serious non-political crimes, or acts contrary to the purposes and principles of the United Nations.

It also provides for minimum standards for the treatment of refugees. They should have access to courts, primary education and papers, including travel documents. The UN High Commissioner for Refugees is charged with supervising the operation of the Convention, and signatories undertake to cooperate in this.

The Refugee Convention is a vital part of human rights machinery in providing at least a basic safety net when individual nation states – which bear the lion's share of responsibility for guaranteeing rights, freedoms and human dignity in their territories – fail in that duty. To undermine it in thought, word and deed, as so many governments have for so much of our still-young century, is to forget or ignore the worst atrocities of the last.

The International Covenants, 1966

The Universal Declaration was always intended to be accompanied by a binding bill of rights in the form of a multinational UN treaty. Rivalry between the Cold War superpowers and disputes about the nature of civil rights on the one hand, and social and economic ones on the other, led to the drafting of two separate instruments representing each half of the human rights whole. The International Covenant on Economic, Social and Cultural Rights and the International Covenant on Civil and Political Rights came into force for the signatory states nine years later.

Each begins with an identical preamble referencing and echoing the assertions in the UN Charter and Universal Declaration as to the 'inherent dignity' and 'equal and inalienable rights' of all humans as 'the foundation of freedom, justice and peace in the world'. The preamble goes on to state the importance of both economic, social and cultural rights as well as civil and political ones and, crucially, to answer an age-old rhetorical challenge about the relationship, or even tension, between individual rights and responsibilities in societies:

> Realizing that the individual, having duties to other individuals and to the community to which he belongs, is under a responsibility to strive for the promotion and observance of the rights recognized in the present Covenant . . .

Article 1 of each Covenant is also identical in recognizing people's self-determination and sovereignty within the framework of international cooperation and law. It is important to remember that international human rights-building might easily have ended in the late 1950s as a result of the polarized ideological positions of mighty eastern and western Blocs. Anti-colonial liberation struggles gave the movement a shot in the arm, but also the need for a narrative that could reflect and respect the aspirations of North and South as well as East and West; of rich and poor countries as well as communist and liberal ones.

Dividing the 'international bill of rights' into two treaties was an attempt to cater for both different political choices and developmental circumstances within a framework of agreed common values. Crucially, economic, social and cultural rights would largely be left to 'progressive realization' over some time and, for the most part, for more political rather than judicial guarantees – 'including particularly the adoption of legislative measures'.

However, the 'jam tomorrow' approach of allowing variation in the pace of progress in different nations was insufficient for civil and political rights. The implication of the International Covenant on Civil and Political Rights is that these freedoms needed to be given immediate effect by 'constitutional processes' and 'such laws as may be necessary'. Thus, the two texts begin to diverge in their second articles. These deal with the means of delivery before the rights themselves are listed.

This distinction has no doubt fuelled some of the more left-wing human rights scepticism of subsequent years. Why should the civil and political right to life be instantly protected by judges, but the right to food be a matter of 'progressive realization' by governments? It is a good and pointed question, no doubt partially answered by the international political wrangling, Cold War and economic polarization of the times when the instruments were drafted and agreed.

Still, there is some logical coherence to the distinction. Independent courts and judges are well placed to examine evidence of individual unlawful killings, better so than elected politicians. They are not, however, qualified for, charged with or reasonably capable of managing the production, conservation and distribution of food in any economy. That said, where states realize their obligations by legislating for food standards, minimum wages or social security, the courts must have their place in guaranteeing the enforcement of these progressive laws.

It is also vital to remember that, notwithstanding distinctions between the two Conventions, both of them prohibit their respective rights being applied in a discriminatory manner on grounds of 'race, colour, sex, language, religion, political or other opinion, national or social origin, property, birth or other status'.

The International Covenant on Economic, Social and Cultural Rights enshrines rights to work and working conditions, including minimum remuneration and a 'decent living' for workers and their families. It guarantees equal pay and conditions for equal work by men and women. It requires safe and healthy working conditions, equal opportunity to promotions and to rest, leisure and reasonable working hours and paid holidays.[2]

It provides rights to form and join trade unions and rights for those trade unions to 'function freely subject to no limitations other than those prescribed by law and which are necessary in a democratic society in the interests of national security or public order or for the protection of the rights and freedoms of others'. It provides for the right to strike and references the earlier International Labour Organization Convention of 1948, governing freedom of association and the right to organize.[3] In many respects, these may be seen as civil and political rights as much as social and economic ones.

It contains a right to social security, protections for the family and especially for children.[4] Marriage must be freely consensual between the spouses and special measures should be taken to protect children, including from discrimination on grounds of parentage. Children should be protected from economic and social exploitation. Interestingly, their employment:

> in work harmful to their morals or health or dangerous to life or likely to hamper their normal development should be punishable by law. States should also set age limits below which the paid employment of child labour should be prohibited and punishable by law.

This more prescriptive and legalistic approach to child exploitation in work again reflects the reality of a blurred line between social and economic rights, including against exploitation, and civil and political rights against inhuman and degrading treatment, forced labour and slavery.

The Convention recognizes the right to an adequate standard of living, including adequate food, clothing, housing and the 'continuous improvement of living conditions' and for 'international co-operation based on free consent . . . to ensure the realization of this right' and 'equitable distribution of world food supplies in relation to need'.[5]

There is a right to the 'highest attainable standard of physical and mental health'. Correspondingly, states have a duty to take steps to reduce stillbirths and infant mortality and improve healthy child development. Similarly, they must seek to improve 'all aspects of environmental and industrial hygiene . . . the prevention, treatment and control of epidemic, endemic, occupational and other diseases', and create 'conditions which would assure to all medical service and medical attention in the event of sickness'.[6]

There is a universal right to education 'directed to the full development of the human personality and the sense of its dignity'. While the 'progressive realization' approach is adopted as elsewhere in the Convention, here it is prescribed in structured stages – free compulsory primary education, then secondary education (in different forms and over time to be provided free to all). Next comes higher education, which 'shall be made equally accessible to all on the basis of capacity by every appropriate means, and in particular by the progressive introduction of free education'. Signatory states undertake to have respect for parents' wishes, including to choose non-state schools (e.g. religious schools), which comply with minimum educational standards.[7]

Finally, there is the right of everyone to 'take part in cultural life', to 'enjoy the benefits of scientific progress and its applications' and to have protection of their intellectual property. States are responsible for 'the conservation, the development and the diffusion of science and culture', undertake to respect the 'freedom indispensable for scientific research and creative activity' and recognize the benefits of international contact and cooperation in these endeavours.[8]

Once more, and regardless of categorization, we see the indivisibility of human rights. Cultural rights are in effect rights to both science and culture. They require associated social and economic rights alongside civil and political liberties to be made real. The obvious need for internationalism in these essential aspects of human endeavour is made explicit.

The International Covenant on Civil and Political Rights begins its list of protections with a guarantee by all signatories to ensure equal access to their enjoyment for all men and women.[9]

A temporary 'get out' or 'derogation' clause is provided for 'time of public emergency which threatens the life of the nation' and which is 'officially proclaimed'. In these circumstances, states may act outside of their ordinary obligations but only 'to the extent strictly required', and without otherwise breaching international law. Importantly, such measures may not involve discrimination 'on the ground of race, colour, sex, language, religion or social origin'. Even in such a state of emergency, states may not derogate from rights to life, against torture, inhuman or degrading treatment, freedom from slavery, debtors' prison and retrospective punishment. The right to recognition as a 'person before the law' and freedom of thought, conscience and religion also enjoy this higher protection.[10]

The right to life under Article 6, however, is not as absolute as it might seem. It is in effect the right to protection of one's life under the law so as not to be 'arbitrarily' deprived of it. It does not even abolish the death penalty 'for the most serious crimes in accordance with the law in force at the time of the commission of the crime', and 'pursuant to a final judgement rendered by a competent court'. Nonetheless, there must always be the possibility of amnesty, pardon or lessening of the death sentence, and it must never be imposed on those below the age of eighteen or pregnant women. It ends:

> Nothing in this article shall be invoked to delay or to prevent the abolition of capital punishment by any State Party to the present Covenant.

It seems that, in 1966, protection from the death penalty was almost as much a matter of 'progressive realization' as protection from starvation. This is hardly surprising, given that the last hangings in the United Kingdom were in 1964 and the death sentence was not formally abolished for all crimes there until the Human Rights Act of 1998. Today fifty-five countries, or a third of the world, have yet to abolish this sentence. Notably, this includes China and the USA.

The rights not to be subjected to torture, or to cruel, inhuman or degrading treatment or punishment and not to be held in slavery or servitude are absolute. That said, there are qualifications on the definition of compulsory work that leave out prison labour or community service and conscription into military service, as long as conscientious objection is provided for.[11]

Then there is the right to liberty and security of the person, protecting people from arbitrary arrest and detention. This is essentially a procedural right with its roots in earlier national instruments that we have considered. Arrested people must be promptly told of the reasons for their arrest and of any criminal charges against them. They must be brought quickly before a judge and entitled to trial or release within a reasonable time. They must have rights to challenge the legality of their detention and, where that is found wanting, to enforceable compensation.[12]

Prisoners 'shall be treated with humanity and with respect'. Those awaiting trial should be separated from convicted people, as should juveniles from adults. Reformation and social rehabilitation are described as the 'essential aim' of prison sentences.[13]

No one shall be imprisoned for 'inability to fulfil a contractual obligation',[14] reminding us of the way in which those unable to pay their debts were incarcerated in workhouses or debtors' prisons, even in western Europe as late as the mid-nineteenth century. I often wonder if the detention of asylum seekers pending decisions on their claims will be viewed with similar shame and disbelief 100 years from now.

Subject to narrow limitations for national security, public order, public health or morals or the rights and freedoms of others, people lawfully within a state should be allowed freedom of movement within it and the right to leave. No one should be 'arbitrarily' refused entry into their own country. Even 'aliens' (as foreign nationals as well as imagined extra-planetary creatures were once described) should not be expelled without some lawful process with the right to be heard.[15]

There is equality before the law and a whole host of familiar criminal due process rights[16] to fair and public hearings, the presumption of innocence, knowledge of the case one faces, time, lawyers and facilities to prepare, and counsel of one's choosing. There must be legal assistance where justice requires this, and the defendant lacks the means. There is a right to call witnesses on one's behalf and to examine those for the prosecution. There must be free interpretation for those who do not understand or speak the language of the court. There should be additional protections for juveniles, and every convicted person should have the right to have their conviction and sentence reviewed by a higher court or tribunal. There is a right to compensation for miscarriages of justice. No one should be tried or punished 'for an offence for which he has already been finally convicted or acquitted in accordance with the law and penal procedure of each country'. There is a rule against retrospective criminalization for behaviour that did not constitute an offence at the relevant time unless it 'was criminal according to the general principles of law recognized by the community of nations'. This caveat has been used to deal with matters such as rape within marriage, which the UK Parliament failed to outlaw, forcing intervention by its highest court as late as 1991.[17]

There is a right 'to recognition everywhere as a person before the law' and protection from 'arbitrary or unlawful interference with . . . privacy, family, home or correspondence' and 'unlawful attacks on' one's 'honour and reputation'.[18]

There is an absolute right to freedom of thought, conscience and religion, with qualifications only permitted for the *manifestations* of that conscience or belief as prescribed in law for the protection of others.[19]

Similarly, while the right to 'hold opinions' is absolute, freedom of expression, as in the 'freedom to seek, receive and impart information and ideas', is subject to such restrictions as are provided by law and necessary for 'respect of the rights or reputations of others' (thus protecting copyright and defamation laws) and 'for the protection of national security or of public order or of public health or morals'.[20] The 'public health or morals' caveat has been increasingly controversial, as has the subsequent provision calling for the prohibition of war propaganda, and advocacy of 'hatred that constitutes incitement to discrimination, hostility or violence'.[21]

For my own part, I find the concept of protecting 'public morals' outmoded beyond much contemporary use. Any public morals justifying a limitation on free expression would surely involve a significant detrimental impact upon 'the rights of others'. Similarly, while laying down our swords and shields 'down by the riverside'[22] is a noble ultimate ambition, such an apparently complete 'war propaganda' prohibition sits uncomfortably alongside the residual lawful justifications for military engagement under the United Nations Charter.[23]

The concepts of 'hatred' and 'incitement to discrimination' seem to me to be perhaps too ill-defined to be of much practical value, even at the high conceptual level of international treaties. Incitement to violence, on the other hand, is well and commonly understood and easily encompassed within both the 'rights of others' and 'protection of public order' qualifications of Article 19, and the regional instruments that flow from it.

The rights of peaceful assembly and freedom of association are protected with only the qualifications for the protection of others allowed in the case of freedom of expression. The right to form and join trade unions and protection for marriage and the family are expressly provided, as in the International Convention on Economic, Social and Cultural Rights. So, once more, we see the conceptual overlap between the two instruments. Marriage must be consensual and there should be equal rights within marriage and on divorce, with appropriate protections for any children. Child protection is to be without discrimination, and to include birth registration and the right to a nationality.[24]

There is the right to participate in politics and elections, including by voting in 'genuine periodic elections which shall be by universal and equal suffrage and shall be held by secret ballot'.[25]

All persons are entitled to equal protection of law without discrimination on grounds 'such as race, colour, sex, language, religion, political or other opinion, national or social origin, property, birth or other status'.[26] Once more, such a broad and open class of potential grounds of discrimination highlights how equal treatment was always intended to be the principal and principled key to the human rights kingdom. People are much less likely to enslave, imprison, monitor, silence or otherwise support the oppression of others if this would apply as much to 'people like them' as to some apparently different group of whoever is currently out of favour.

Finally, there is protection for 'ethnic, religious or linguistic minorities' to enjoy their own culture, religion and language.[27] Some people talk about a tension between 'group rights' and 'individual rights'. I argue that all rights and freedoms reflect us as both individuals and social creatures to our core. Similarly, different categories of rights are indivisible, as demonstrated by the way that cultural rights require both social and economic investment and civil and political protection.

With Part IV of each of the two global conventions, the 'enforcement' mechanism diverges. Still, both may seem less than ideal to those used to the faster bite and sharper teeth of national law. In both cases, signatory states undertake to submit reports to the UN Secretary-General as to their progress on delivering the rights and freedoms contained within the two halves of the 'International Bill of Rights'. At this point, various organs of the UN take responsibility for reviewing and pronouncing on that progress. However, the possibility of inter-state complaints and dispute resolution before an inevitably highly contested and elected Human Rights Committee is reserved for the *Civil* Rights Convention only.

Few on any side of the human rights argument would suggest that these complex supra-national mechanisms are the best way to deliver day-to-day protection for the world's population. However, we cannot have our cake and eat it. We cannot plead the greater cultural proximity and democratic legitimacy of local, national and continental government, while simultaneously castigating international – and essentially diplomatic – institutions for lacking the ultimate power properly to hold them to account. This conundrum lies at the heart of any attempt at 'global governance' in our shrinking interconnected world.

Regional Human Rights Treaties

Many an imaginative child's first letter signs off with an expansive home address going well beyond their zip code. Short of the solar system and somewhere between the nation and the world, sits the continent. If there were ever any doubt about the direct connection between justice and peace, the 1930s had ended it. This was especially so in Europe where two world wars had begun. So, it is unsurprising that those seeking to rebuild the lands of Milton, Molière, Mozart and Michelangelo should have made the enterprise of cooperating around enforceable human rights a priority.

Churchill's 1942 letter to Archbishop William Temple and much more of his wartime commentary revealed a desire for human rights to be at the heart of the post-war world. In this ambition he was far from alone in Britain or in Europe. In May

1948 he attended the Congress of Europe at The Hague alongside François Mitterrand, Konrad Adenauer and academic, business, civil society and trade union leaders. They called for a charter of rights and, vitally, a court to enforce them.

No doubt there were always some who saw the resulting Council of Europe as one step towards a federal future. But a greater number saw it as a means of embedding democracy and the rule of law – of which rights and freedoms are part – in their recovering continent. Thus it would be protected from totalitarianism of right or left. So when the Council was founded by the Treaty of London in 1949, the drafting of what would become the 1950 Convention for the Protection of Human Rights and Fundamental Freedoms was at the top of the agenda.

The twelve original member states[28] sent 100 parliamentarians to Strasbourg in the summer of 1949, and British Conservative MP Sir David Maxwell Fyfe (also a Nuremberg prosecutor) led the initial framing process with French former Minister and Resistance fighter Pierre-Henri Teitgen. After detailed drafting by a committee of experts, the Convention (commonly known as the European Convention on Human Rights or ECHR) was opened for signing in Rome in 1950. It came into force in September 1953.

The Convention, which focuses on civil and political rights, is in three parts, with the rights and freedoms themselves listed in the first.

Article 1 places the duty of securing the rights and freedoms to everyone within their respective jurisdictions to the contracting states in the Council of Europe.

Article 2 protects the right to life. It prohibits intentional killing save pursuant to a court sentence for a capital crime, or where the use of lethal force was 'no more than absolutely necessary' to protect a person from unlawful violence, effect a lawful arrest, prevent the escape of a lawful detainee or in lawful action to quell a riot. It is worth noting the test of 'absolute necessity'. It is deliberately far stricter than ordinary 'necessity' with its usual human rights companion 'proportionality', before an interference with the right may be justified.

Article 3 provides that 'no one shall be subjected to torture or to inhuman or degrading treatment or punishment'. It is the shortest provision in the Convention and intended to provide the most absolute protection, with no exceptions whatsoever. However, inevitably, it has periodically begged questions as to how bad intention, treatment and harm have to be in order to meet the thresholds of 'inhuman or degrading treatment' or 'torture'.[29]

Article 4 provides absolute protection from slavery and servitude. It also prohibits forced or compulsory labour. However, this excludes prison work, military service (and conscientious objector alternatives), service 'exacted in case of an emergency or calamity threatening the life or well-being of the community' and that 'which forms part of normal civic obligations'. The various caveats indicate once more that the strongest protection lies in the obligation on states to prevent people enslaving each other, and not to discriminate in the imposition of various service obligations which states themselves may from time to time impose.

Article 5 provides the right to liberty and security of the person. It resonates loudly with much earlier national rights instruments such as Magna Carta, the French Declaration and the US Bill of Rights. No one shall be deprived of their liberty, save where legally prescribed in one of six cases. However, these are as tightly constrained as is possible in a high-level international treaty and in contrast with the more loosely defined exceptions to balanced or 'qualified' (as opposed to procedural) rights that come later in the Convention. The closed list of justifications for lawful detention are: following a court conviction; for non-compliance with a court order; lawful arrest to bring someone before a criminal court; the educational supervision of children; quarantine for infectious diseases or the detention of 'persons of unsound mind, alcoholics or drug addicts or vagrants'; and detention to prevent illegal entry into a country or with a view to deportation or extradition.

The lengthy article then goes on to provide the procedural protections afforded to everyone lawfully detained on one of the grounds previously set out. They must be informed 'promptly' and in a language they understand of the reasons for their arrest and any charges against them. Criminal arrestees must be brought promptly before a judge, and entitled to trial within a reasonable time or release pending their trial. Any detained person must be entitled to challenge the legality of their detention. This should be decided 'speedily' by a court which must also release anyone held unlawfully. In contrast with other rights and freedoms, there is an express and enforceable right to compensation for anyone held in breach of Article 5.

Article 6 details the content of the right to a fair trial, whether in relation to civil rights or criminal charges. In both cases this includes a right to a fair and public hearing within a 'reasonable time by an independent and impartial tribunal established by law'. Judgements should be public, but the press and public may be excluded from all or part of a trial for specific reasons. These are the interests of morals, public order or national security, the protection of juveniles or the privacy of the parties, or to the extent 'strictly necessary' to protecting the interests of justice.

Those charged with criminal offences shall be presumed

innocent until proven guilty and have five minimum procedural rights provided to them:

- They must have prompt and detailed information of the accusation they face in a language they understand.
- They must have adequate time and facilities to prepare their defence.
- They should be allowed to defend themselves in person or with legal assistance which they choose, and free assistance if they lack sufficient funds and justice requires this.
- They must be able to cross-examine their accusers and to obtain the attendance and examination of supportive witnesses on the same terms as the prosecution.
- They must have free interpreter assistance if they cannot understand or speak the language of the court.

Article 7 provides the additional justice protection that no one shall be convicted of an offence that was not criminal at the time it was committed. Nor should a heavier penalty be retrospectively imposed. Nonetheless, as discussed in the context of the International Convention on Civil and Political Rights, there is an exception where, at the time the 'act or omission' was committed, it 'was criminal according to the general principles of law recognised by civilised nations'. This may seem to some a considerable loophole or weakness in the protection from retrospective criminal penalization. Yet, one can see how it might be an important ethical safeguard against citizens of rogue states believing that these tyrannies may grant indefinite impunity for active cooperation in the vilest crimes against humanity.

The first paragraph of Article 8 provides that 'everyone has the right to respect for his private and family life, his home and his correspondence'. In what becomes the template for the next few balanced rights, its second paragraph contains a qualification and attempts to explain how this may be met:

> There shall be no interference by a public authority with the exercise of this right except such as is in accordance with the law and is necessary in a democratic society in the interests of national security, public safety or the economic well-being of the country, for the prevention of disorder or crime, for the protection of health or morals, or for the protection of the rights and freedoms of others.

European jurists, including in the European Court of Human Rights set up in Strasbourg as the custodian of the Convention, have long regarded it as a 'living instrument' capable of keeping up with the times. This sits in sharp contrast with some, for example American conservatives who prefer the 'originalist' or more literal and fundamentalist approach to the interpretation of their Bill of Rights. Thus, the broad concept of 'private and family life, his home and correspondence' has inevitably been one of the provisions that is most capable of development over time.

This evolution has kept up with changing cultural and democratic attitudes to notions of legitimate and lawful love and intimacy, increased migration and technological revolution. Originalist-style 'hawks', including in Britain, have periodically found it objectionable that a 1950 idea of 'private and family life' should have been organic enough to protect same-sex loving relationships and cross-border families over time. They have baulked at 'private life' and indeed 'correspondence' now including electronic communications and mountains of digital personal data. Yet living-instrument 'doves' believe that the ability of the Convention to be applied to changing times constitutes an enormous strength, not a weakness. Far older national laws have been capable of similar reinterpretation for the prevailing circumstances. Further, the caveats that justify interference with Article 8 rights, including the elastic 'rights and freedoms of others', are also broadly cast and capable of contemporary application.

Article 9 deals with freedom of thought, conscience and religion. Its two clauses provide firstly for this absolute right, including 'to change' religion or belief. Then comes the qualified right 'either alone or in community with others and in public or private, to manifest' religion or belief, 'in worship, teaching, practice and observance'. It is only the *manifestation* that may be subject to limitations that are prescribed by law and 'necessary in a democratic society in the interests of public safety, for the protection of public order, health or morals, or for the protection of the rights and freedoms of others'.

Once more we see the 'necessary in a democratic society' test. This has been interpreted over many years to include a notion of 'proportionality' between the legitimate societal objective pursued and the corresponding interference with rights. Necessary and proportionate interference with qualified rights, alongside the golden rule against discrimination, are the very antithesis of any notion of an 'end justifying the means'.

Article 10 protects freedom of expression. Once more it is broadly cast as a right 'to hold opinions and to receive and impart information and ideas without interference by public authority and regardless of frontiers'.

Interestingly, the 'licensing of broadcasting, television or cinema enterprises' is expressly allowed, presumably to draw a distinction between emergent and potentially pervasive communication technologies in relatively few hands (at a time of limited 'frequencies', 'studios' and 'cinemas') and the by then over 500-year-old ubiquitous printing press. When a powerful communications technology is structurally monopolistic there are more obviously democratic grounds for licensing it. But even a permissible licensing regime must itself comply with the strictures of Article 10.

However absolutist we might feel about free speech and expression, in truth it can never be totally without qualification. Even the legendary First Amendment of the US Bill of Rights, though at first glance unqualified, has necessarily been interpreted by the Supreme Court to allow, for example, the prohibition of obscenity,[30] incitement to imminent violence,[31] and violations of intellectual property.[32] The much later drafters of Article 10 of the ECHR faced up to such issues from the outset with its second paragraph. The 'exercise of these freedoms' is described as coming with 'duties and responsibilities' and 'may be subject to such formalities, conditions and restrictions or penalties as are prescribed by law and are necessary in a democratic society' for listed reasons. These are:

> in the interests of national security, territorial integrity or public safety, for the prevention of disorder or crime, for the protection of health or morals, for the protection of the reputation or rights of others, for preventing the disclosure of information received in confidence, or for maintaining the authority and impartiality of the judiciary.

As with the rights to respect for privacy and manifestation of conscience in the previous two articles, we see the test of proportionate necessity and the requirement that limitations are 'prescribed by law'. This need for adequate prior prescription by way of clearly accessible regulation provides a platform for democratic scrutiny and a safeguard against arbitrary, discriminatory and disproportionate interference with the right. It is one of the many ways in which democracy and the rule of law play partnership roles in guaranteeing the rights which are in turn essential to them both.

Article 11 protects the right to freedom of peaceful assembly and to freedom of association with others, including the right to form and to join trade unions. Once more it comes with a caveat, allowing legally prescribed limitations that are necessary in a democratic society on grounds of national security, public safety, prevention of disorder or crime, the protection of health, morals or the rights and freedoms of others.

Article 12 grants a right to 'men and women of marriageable age' to marry and found a family, according to the national laws governing the exercise of this right. The variables of 'marriageable age' and governing 'national laws' are arguably so vague as to make the right soft enough to be relatively toothless but for the broad and dynamic nature of Article 8. It is the earlier article that has been such a driver in protecting married and non-married families of different races, nationalities and sexualities, since the founding of the Convention.

In Articles 2 to 7, we have seen protections for the individual human, even if living an essentially isolated existence. They are to be shielded from arbitrary killing, from inhuman treatment, slavery and unfair penalization of various types. In Articles 8 to 12, we begin to see human rights reflecting social creatures. They live in families, other intimate relationships and faith communities. They want to receive and impart opinions and even act on the same in concert with others. I have been reading this Convention all of my adult life, yet still marvel at the sheer poetic insight of its post-war drafters.

Article 13 of the Convention provides the right to an 'effective remedy' at the national level for everyone whose rights and freedoms have been violated. This effectively means that Council of Europe (a larger group than the EU) signatory states must ensure that their various laws and justice institutions provide effective protection and redress for Convention rights.

Since 2000, the United Kingdom has attempted to guarantee this compliance by way of the Human Rights Act 1998.[33] This incorporates the various substantive rights into domestic law and provides a framework for public authorities – including courts – to give them direct effect. UK courts must take Strasbourg Court jurisprudence 'into account' in their decisions, but they are not bound by it.

All domestic legislation, with a recent exception in the form of the Illegal Migration Act 2023[34] (designed to facilitate the Rishi Sunak Conservative Government's plan to deter small boats and transport asylum seekers to Rwanda), must 'so far as is possible' be interpreted compatibly with Convention rights. Where this is not possible (because domestic statutes are too clearly incompatible), domestic law remains in operation while the higher courts make a 'declaration of incompatibility'. This declaration has only moral and persuasive force in effectively suggesting that Parliament (in practice, the Government) think again.

This is a constitutional compromise designed to balance the relationship between democracy and the rule of law; between parliament and both domestic and international courts. It may be described as a *dialogue* approach to delivering rights and freedoms, in contrast with the shouting matches that have so often dominated the politics and political commentary of the early twenty-first century.

Article 14 of the ECHR provides the all-important protection from discrimination in the delivery of the other Convention provisions. It is hugely powerful both ethically and legally in preventing dominant elites or indeed majorities in any member state from persecuting unpopular or otherwise vulnerable minorities. Crucially, there need not be an actual violation of the substantive right (to liberty or privacy, etc.) for this provision to be breached. If law or policy operates *in the realm of* another right or freedom, it must do so in an even-handed and non-discriminatory manner. Further, the grounds of discrimination are not closed. Sex, race, colour, language, religion, political or other opinion, national or social origin, association with a national minority, property, birth or other status are given only as examples of the potentially vulnerable groupings.

Article 15 provides the exception or 'derogation' clause for 'time of war or other public emergency threatening the life of the nation'. Once more, such exceptions must only be those 'strictly required by the exigencies of the situation' and not inconsistent with other international law obligations. No derogation is allowed from protections against inhuman and degrading treatment or torture or from slavery. The right to life may only be derogated from as regards 'lawful acts of war'.

Section 2 of the Convention establishes the Court of Human Rights which renders the ECHR one of the most effective international human rights mechanisms in the world. Section 3 deals with miscellaneous procedural matters. Then there are a number of protocols to the Convention adding other protections in the years after its original signing. In Paris in 1952, the First Protocol added peaceful enjoyment of property,[35] rights to education[36] and free elections.[37] In Vilnius in 2002, signatories to the Thirteenth Protocol finally abolished the death penalty 'in all circumstances', including in time of war.

Following its invasion of Ukraine, Russia was suspended from the Council of Europe in February 2022. On 15 March, Russia gave formal notice of withdrawal to have effect in December, but was instead expelled with immediate effect the next day. At the time of writing there remain forty-six member states.

The American Declaration of the Rights and Duties of Man preceded even the Universal Declaration by around eight months in 1948. Still, it wasn't until late 1969 that the American Convention on Human Rights (ACHR) was signed in San José, Costa Rica. It was not brought into force by the Organization of American States (OAS) until the summer of 1978. The Inter-American Human Rights system comprises both a Commission and a Court. The former is charged with promoting and reporting on human rights in signatory states, and also performs a supporting and interlocutory role to the Court.

The Convention is highly reminiscent of the International Covenant on Civil and Political Rights in particular (life, humane treatment, fair trials, privacy, conscience, assembly, etc.). Considerably less attention is given to social, economic and cultural matters. These were bolstered ten years later in the 1988 Protocol of San Salvador (adding the rights to work, health, food, education, etc.). The Second Protocol of 1990 attempts to restrict the use of the death penalty, but this has only been ratified by thirteen of the thirty-five members of the OAS.

Indeed, the Convention itself is only currently ratified by twenty-four states. Trinidad and Tobago denounced the Convention in 1998 over the death penalty issue. Venezuela denounced the Convention in 2012 and re-ratified it seven years later. In contrast with other international human rights conventions, church influence means the right to life in the ACHR expressly applies 'from the moment of conception', causing pro-choice (and significant OAS funder) Canada not to ratify it, even with the possibility of a reservation.

Despite President Jimmy Carter having signed it and the headquarters of the OAS being in Washington DC, the USA has never ratified this human rights treaty of the Americas. Objections to doing so include the rights of individual US states under the Constitution, US national sovereignty and concerns around both abortion and the death penalty.

The African Charter on Human and Peoples' Rights (also known as the Banjul Charter) was adopted in 1981 and came into force in 1986. It is the human rights treaty of the African Union[38] (previously the Organisation of African Unity) and is enforced by a Commission and a Court, the first judges of which were elected in 2006. As the youngest of the three continental human rights treaties, it contains both civil and political and social, economic and cultural rights reminiscent of the global conventions. However, in keeping with African communitarian tradition and experience, it also frames some more newly conceived post-colonial 'peoples' rights'. These include the rights of peoples to have equality and freedom from domination,[39] self-determination,[40] freedom to dispose of natural resources,[41] rights to development,[42] peace and security,[43] and a generally satisfactory environment.[44]

In its Article 29, it is more explicit about the role of an individual's duties than in the various caveats to rights and freedoms in earlier instruments. These are listed as:

> 1. To preserve the harmonious development of the family and to work for the cohesion and respect of the family; to respect his parents at all times, to maintain them in case of need;

2. To serve his national community by placing his physical and intellectual abilities at its service;
3. Not to compromise the security of the State whose national or resident he is;
4. To preserve and strengthen social and national solidarity, particularly when the latter is threatened;
5. To preserve and strengthen the national independence and the territorial integrity of his country and to contribute to its defence in accordance with the law;
6. To work to the best of his abilities and competence, and to pay taxes imposed by law in the interest of the society;
7. To preserve and strengthen positive African cultural values in his relations with other members of the society, in the spirit of tolerance, dialogue and consultation and, in general, to contribute to the promotion of the moral well being of society;
8. To contribute to the best of his abilities, at all times and at all levels, to the promotion and achievement of African unity.

The United Nations Convention against Torture, 1984

In addition to the two global Conventions on Civil and Political and Social, Economic and Cultural Rights, the UN has become the custodian of a number of subsequent issue-specific treaties with attempted worldwide reach.

The Convention against Torture and Other Cruel, Inhuman or Degrading Treatment or Punishment (UNCAT) was adopted by the General Assembly on 10 December (Human Rights Day) 1984 and came into force on 26 June 1987. At the time of writing, the Convention has attracted 173 state signatories. A combination of its coverage and gravity has caused its absolute prohibitions of the cruellest treatment to be accepted as a principle of 'customary international law', binding all states whether they have ratified or domesticated them or not.

Article 1 defines torture as the intentional infliction of physical or mental suffering for a number of reasons or any reason when by a public official. The Convention then provides for an absolute ban on torture and removes any possible recourse to the excuse of 'just following orders' by those in a chain of command. It includes a ban on states sending people to places of torture (whether by return or other expulsion or extradition), and a duty to prosecute or extradite those guilty of this ultimate human rights sin.

Anti-Discrimination Treaties

The post-war years have also seen the drafting, signing and promotion of a number of treaties addressing internationally experienced forms of profound discrimination, subsequently monitored by UN Committees. The principal instruments in this category are the 1965 Convention on the Elimination of Racial Discrimination (CERD), the 1979 Convention on the Elimination of All Forms of Discrimination against Women (CEDAW), the 1989 Convention on the Rights of the Child (CRC) and the 2006 Convention on the Rights of Persons with Disabilities (CRPD).

The CERD was adopted in 1965 after much understandable wrangling about the distinctions between race and religion, and the balance between combatting racial hatred and protecting free speech. Despite widespread ratification (with some reservations), Article 4's requirement to criminalize 'all dissemination of ideas based on racial superiority or hatred, incitement to racial discrimination, as well as all acts of violence or incitement to such acts' remains controversial in both theory and application to this day.

The CEDAW requires state parties to enshrine gender equality in their domestic laws and enables 'special measures' such as affirmative action to accelerate equality between men and women. These are not to be regarded as discrimination in themselves. It obliges signatories to take action against the trafficking of women and prostitution and mandates that states take action to advance sex equality in a range of key areas of civil, political, social, economic and cultural life.

The CRC is the equivalent international treaty for the protection of children, defined as under eighteen years old. It is a vital human rights document, not least for emphasizing the manner in which personhood is not triggered by maturity, citizenship, or some other form of acquired status. It puts 'the best interests of the child' at its heart, while balancing the special role of parents, in child protection and development, with that of the state.

The CRPD was the first international human rights treaty of the twenty-first century and was adopted by the General Assembly in December 2006. In contrast with traditional charity, paternalism, abjection and even more sinister overmedicalization, it attempts to achieve full equality, dignity and autonomy for people with disabilities. It was an early focal point of the developing movement for disability rights, importantly introducing 'reasonable accommodation' or adjustment for people's differential needs.

This is our imperfect but vital twenty-first-century human rights inheritance, crafted by the survivors of the Second Great

War, in order better to protect fundamental freedoms and consequential peace thereafter. It is worth having some familiarity with its main provisions, if only so as to argue about its adequacy and application more effectively. As we will see, these arguments come thick and fast.

3.
Trojan Horse or Human Shield?

I fear the Greeks even when bearing gifts.

Laocoön, *The Aeneid*, Virgil

Having laid some foundations and drawn the basic architecture of human rights, it now feels important to test them a little, to subject what I believe to be self-evidently valuable to some extremely common and trenchant criticisms. The first is the notion that rights in general, but positive state duties and social and economic rights in particular, form a Trojan horse[1] for a kind of dangerous, undercover, left-wing politics. The argument goes that instead of taking their chances in an honest marketplace of manifestos that win or lose at the ballot box, human rights defenders resort to a kind of fake neutrality or 'anti-politics'. Worse still, they deliberately dress up extremely radical and contentious ideas with the disguise of universalism.

This depiction is often accompanied by a suggestion that the law should only really protect us from the state's undue interference into our lives, and never address cases of the authorities' neglect. Some advocates of this position are more than happy to defend so-called first generation freedoms from torture, slavery, arbitrary detention, unfair trials, undue surveillance and censorship. However, they draw the line at any positive duties upon those who govern, especially when this has implications for public expenditure and taxation.[2]

Under this analysis, the rule against torture would still outlaw abusive police interrogation methods, but it would not require the state to investigate and prevent modern-day slavery. This, notwithstanding the history of just how much aggressive state intervention was required to outlaw the original transatlantic trade.

It would grant us our 'day in court' when arrested under suspicion or accused of a serious crime. *Habeas corpus* (liberating unlawfully detained people) is superficially extolled without the vaguest irony by many a human rights sceptic, who, despite their contemporary nationalism, prefers law in the dead imperial language of Latin. Some would further support our right to a fair trial if we were facing the loss of our property or reputation. Still, such a trial might be conducted without affordable, qualified legal representation.

Positive Obligations

The rights sceptic's aversion to positive obligations is as incoherent as it is chauvinistic. How on earth is a society to protect even the most basic civil liberties without, at the very least, a functioning police service, court and justice system – including legal aid for those facing the greatest jeopardy with the least resources? If you agree to create such a system with a view to establishing a rule of law that is real and not illusory, how could it work if the authorities are not under some positive duties to enforce the law, including with an even hand and without corruption, abuse and neglect?

The treatment of rape victims anywhere in the world is an

obvious case in point. It is a clear litmus test for the strength of any civilized society, not least as we understand that in times of war and other societal breakdown incident and impunity rise exponentially. When I was a young lawyer in the UK, in spite of the importance of historically embedded fair trial rights in our jurisdictions, our state was found wanting by the European Convention system for allowing men accused of rape tactically to sack their legal teams at particular moments. They could then cross-examine their alleged victims in person, including about irrelevant aspects of their past intimate lives. Sometimes this would go on for days on end at the famous Old Bailey, the Central Criminal Court in London.

Despite the general proposition that a defendant should have a choice over their counsel and even the right to represent themselves, this was seen, rightly in my view, as potentially inhuman and degrading treatment for complainants. Inevitably, some of them must have been genuine victims of rape. The original abuse and trauma were too easily repeated by way of a public trial in which the alleged violator was given free rein.

Understandably, anxious judges were concerned not to be too proscriptive over a litigant in person accused of one of the gravest crimes. Thanks to the impact of human rights thinking, that loophole for abuse was narrowed, and cross-examination by a defendant in person was ruled out in these cases.

In subsequent decades, we have come to understand much more about what it takes for victims of sexual abuse in particular to survive and recover enough to lead healthy, positive and contented lives, even before any brave attempt at seeking redress for the crimes committed against them. At the very least, policing, prosecution and courts systems should be staffed with personnel adequately trained not to exacerbate trauma by disproportionate disbelief, delay and intrusion. Psychological injury may take considerably more time and resource to heal than physical scars. Those who have been harmed in their own homes need new and safe ones to find refuge. Sometimes they require ongoing protection from their predators. Achieving any or all of this, while nonetheless guaranteeing vital fair trials to those accused, takes sensitivity, balanced judgement and public investment.

Further, even without constant reference to the now long-established international human rights agreements to do more, complex modern societies often make political and legislative decisions to outlaw various forms of discrimination between people. Some go even further, to provide a safety net, rope ladder or something even more substantial, in the areas of health, education, shelter and wealth inequality. Public officials undoubtedly have positive obligations to operate these systems in the way that voters and legislators intended, and are entitled to expect.

Public Law

A common argument is that too many rules and too much 'red tape' inevitably lead to 'kritocracy' – a *rule of lawyers and judges* – not the rule of law. I agree that the cost of applying umpteen adversarial hearings and appeals, with legal representation for every healthcare or welfare benefit decision, could end up costing as much as or more than the precious and contested support itself. Nonetheless, discretion without properly enforced rules, particularly in the realm of public spending, while avoiding 'kritocracy', may facilitate 'kleptocracy' instead. As we have seen in many countries, including during the Covid-19 pandemic, under this kind of government by theft and corruption, those in power give public contracts, grants and other pecuniary benefits to their friends and family, instead of to those with the best goods and services, or in the greatest need.

Conversely, clear rules and a viable appeal system in these areas of public administration, like properly enforced laws in the private sphere, will help service-users themselves and first-instance decision-makers of integrity argue for ethical and legally sound choices from within. This was certainly my own experience as a young Government lawyer in the 1990s during the blossoming of British judicial review of administrative action, and before the reduction and destruction of civil legal aid. This area of law has long been denigrated by many elected politicians of all stripes. Nonetheless, if the rule of law and human rights in no small part prevent and provide redress against abuses of power, government as well as individuals, charities and corporations must surely be held to account.

'The Judge over my shoulder'[3] was often a better guide than the Minister in my face. Like most other public servants whom I met during my time in the UK Home Office before the turn of the century, my ambition was to help people access their rights and freedoms, not to catch them out for the late filing of a form, or incomplete, painful and embarrassing disclosure of poverty, persecution or other frailty. It is easy for politicians to be cynical about the immigration, welfare and housing lawyers who act for those who are especially dependent on the state. This cynicism slips effortlessly into hostility unless you have known what it is to have been roughly treated and have nowhere else to turn.

The state infrastructure and public spending needed to provide genuine access to justice makes this bundle of protections the bridge between civil and political and social and economic rights. It is also the link between negative and positive state obligations. Accordingly, if justice is not paid for, treasured and guaranteed, no other rights and freedoms can be made real. As we move deeper into the more obvious territory of social rights rather than procedural justice, the arguments and dilemmas are perhaps even more acute.

The Parable of the Pandemic

If ever there were a parable for almost every inequality on the planet, it was the Covid-19 pandemic. This was declared a Public Health Emergency of International Concern by the World Health Organization on 30 January 2020. What followed was simultaneously dystopian to untrained eyes and to some extent all too predictable to those in the international scientific community who had long placed such a disaster on the register of global risk.[4]

Worldwide deaths exceeded 6.5 million as governments scrambled to produce and acquire sufficient protective and ventilation equipment and medicines. Ultimately, life-saving vaccines emerged via a predictable combination of high-level collaboration and fierce competition between the richest powers in particular.

Western democracies enacted some of the harshest restrictions on civil liberties in living or even recorded memory. Perhaps inevitably, given the scale and speed of the emergency, these were observed and enforced with a less than even hand. There were high-profile cases of lockdown violations by the powerful alongside abuses of police power against some of the most vulnerable. In the UK, Cabinet Ministers and their most senior advisers were found to have breached their own guidance. Conversely, elderly people died and grieved in isolation. Thirty-three-year-old Sarah Everard was kidnapped, raped and murdered by an off-duty police officer purporting to arrest her as she walked home in a London suburb. The police used social distancing rules to brutally break up a peaceful vigil held in response.[5]

While debates around the origins and handling of the pandemic will rage for many years, there was significant scientific and political consensus about the need for some proportionate if severe restrictions upon liberties to protect lives. Yet, while it may have been necessary, pandemic authoritarianism was hopelessly asymmetric in a number of ways.

Social distancing was often strictly enforced against individuals, families and small businesses, but far less so on the construction sites, in the call centres and warehouses of corporate giants. Normal government procurement rules were relaxed in the attempt to secure vital equipment, but there was relatively little compulsory requisitioning or rationing, creating considerable opportunity for profiteering and corruption.

In the UK, there was temporary housing for a significant proportion of homeless people, but little compulsory acquisition of large vacant residential, industrial or commercial leisure property to allow all the poorest people to experience safe, healthier and happier lockdowns. At a graphic if micro level, we witnessed heart-warming gestures of social solidarity by many people towards the most vulnerable of their neighbours. Others gifted us bizarre and unforgettable online images of their aggressive panic-buying of dried pasta and toilet paper. For future generations, these may come to symbolize the desperate consumerism of a world in crisis.

Those required to work in health, cleaning and other

essential public services did so at great personal risk before mass vaccination. When those critical vaccines arrived, as a result of large-scale public and philanthropic investment, normal rules on intellectual property were not promptly and temporarily waived to allow them to be shared at scale and genuine production cost with millions of people in the Global South. It was as if Big Pharma was refusing to share the floor plan locating emergency exits in a burning building, even though governments, charities and altruistic scientists had collaborated to build those fire escapes in the first place.

Dead bodies floated down the sacred Ganges River[6] while subcontracted Indian manufacturers provided vaccines to be sent to the West.[7] If ever there were a justification for human rights principles to be applied more directly and effectively to international institutions and corporations, it was this.

Inevitably, long periods of enforced curfew favoured those who could live off capital and savings rather than non-existent or stagnant wages. While in many economies, significant payments were made to fund the basic existence of those unable to work and trade, in too much of the world, these were not often enough put directly into the hands of workers, as opposed to their erstwhile and occasionally fraudulent employers. Further, as restrictions began to ease, there seemed to be little political advocacy for the wealthiest individuals and corporations to bear more of the debt burden, nor for the kind of civil, social and economic resets that followed World War II all over the globe.

Healthy, Wealthy and Wise

However, just as justice and security inevitably dominated so much political debate after 9/11, healthcare inevitably became a central pressing political issue during this emergency. Perhaps this was not before time. Medical care had been framed as a human right in the Universal Declaration in 1948. Two years earlier, in the preamble to the Constitution of the World Health Organization – another vital part of post-war international architecture – health was also described in holistic terms:

> Health is a state of complete physical, mental, and social well-being and not merely the absence of disease or infirmity.

Of course, the International Covenant on Economic, Social and Cultural Rights requires the progressive realization of the 'highest attainable standard of physical and mental health'. This leaves a great deal of room for developmental, regional, local, political and economic differences about how the goal should be achieved.[8]

Canada is seen as a model for a National Health Insurance system: funded by taxation but delivered independently of the state. Germany and a number of other European countries chose a path of social health insurance via a payroll tax. The US and the UK are often seen as polar opposite paradigms for population-wide healthcare provision. The former embraces a private insurance model, with much of the financing coming as an employment benefit to those fortunate enough to be in the right kind of prized stable employment. In the post-war period, the latter – via its separate health jurisdictions in England, Scotland, Wales and Northern Ireland, boosted by influxes of skilled staff from first the Commonwealth and then Europe – began building a National Health Service (NHS). This was to be universal, free at the point of need and funded by general taxation.

At this point I must be honestly partisan and more than a

little patriotic. The American private profit model is the most expensive in the world. It still leaves swathes of the population without even basic coverage in their greatest need.[9] This is exacerbated by the similar prioritization of private profit in other aspects of social policy, such as not requiring US employers to give a single day's paid maternity leave to their staff. By contrast and despite well over a decade of austerity and other forms of undermining by stealth and design,[10] I believe the NHS to be among the greatest progressive political experiments in world history.

Nonetheless, even this visionary model only highlights the gaps and contradictions inherent in the current version of the UK's wider welfare state. At the time of writing, we are experiencing a national crisis in social and end of life care for the generation that survived both World War II and the Covid-19 pandemic. Such is the gravity of the situation that the Archbishop of Canterbury, Justin Welby, devoted his New Year's message and a significant Church of England report[11] to the subject in January 2023:

> We know our care system is broken: but it doesn't have to be. We can rise to the challenge of fixing it . . . Caring goes to the heart of what it means to be human. It's hard, but it can also be the most life-giving thing we ever do. It comes back to that essential lesson: we need each other.

This failure of the state to provide vital care on a societal scale is in turn putting the social and economic advancement of the now middle-aged daughters, in particular, of the elderly in jeopardy. If your eighty-year-old parent is suffering from cancer, the NHS will still aspire to provide treatment and care, including hospitalization when necessary. If their chronic diagnosis is one of dementia, essential at-home or residential care will incur significant family cost, debt and could even be non-existent. Notwithstanding the obvious illogic, discrimination and cruelty of this outcome, human rights to health and dignity will not save the day without lasting political consensus.

Food for Thought

Universal secondary school education was a clear and early social and economic rights priority for the post-war international community. In most developed nations this has involved severely limiting child labour, legal requirements for children to attend school, and for parents to secure that attendance. In poorer societies there have been valuable experiments in providing financial incentives to parents to prioritize their children's education over the work and financial contribution that they might otherwise make to hard-pressed families.

In all cases, in exchange for the limitation on parental and child freedom, we must expect certain duties on the state and its entrusted educators to protect, care for and educate children and young people adequately during the school day. Human rights laws protect children of different sexes, races, faiths and abilities from unlawful discrimination, even while allowing room for heated social and political debate about sex, faith, and financial and ability-based school entry policies. Within the Council of Europe, these laws have outlawed corporal punishment in school and provide other protections from neglect and abuse by those in charge of our children. And voters demand decent school buildings, facilities, books and resources.

Yet, even in some of the wealthiest countries, there are large numbers of children who regularly go to school hungry and without a decent packed or school lunch, or the means to buy one. This may be more than one in eight children in the United States, with the number having fallen due to federal government interventions during the pandemic, only to rise again once normal service began to be resumed.[12] In the United Kingdom, and regardless of its welfare state, as many as a third of school-aged children may be experiencing this level of food insecurity.[13]

These figures demonstrate abject failure in the progressive realization of the right to adequate living standards and food under the International Covenant on Economic, Social and Cultural Rights, even as we approach its fifth decade in force. Furthermore, whatever one says about the adequacy of the minimum wages and benefits payments to parents juggling food, clothing, housing and energy bills, how can children's rights to secondary education be fulfilled without the provision of food, alongside teaching, shelter and physical security during the school day?

Any number of studies over recent years have demonstrated the effect of nutrition on a young person's behaviour and academic performance. Further, to eat together or apart is an obvious way of including or excluding people from small units of society, whether in the family, at work or in other social life. School is supposed to be a preparation for this.

I once attended a Central London school lunch at the request of an inspirational head teacher who wanted her many deprived pupils to learn how to use cutlery, make conversation and share communal dishes with each other and their occasional guests. What a contrast with so many schools where some children will eat meals of varying nutritional value brought from home (thus exposing their differing family circumstances), some will have money or free meal tokens with which to make good and bad nutritional choices, and others will have nothing at all. This is discrimination in the most formative years.

There is something fundamentally wrong with limited and complex entitlements to school food for children who are compelled to be in education rather than work, and who do not receive financial payments, except indirectly through their parents. Yet, I cannot currently point to a single binding or even persuasive legal precedent pointing to a clear consequential rights violation. Instead, these vital human rights of a necessarily disenfranchised minority have been largely left to politics to address and often ignore.

So notwithstanding loud claims to the contrary, Troy would seem to be more than safe from any impending invasion by the Greeks.

Human Wrongs?

There are also prevalent and fierce criticisms that human rights actually prop up a political and economic status quo of obscene levels of entrenched global inequality. Human rights are said to protect the property interests of the super-wealthy from any serious attempts at radical social and economic adjustment. Some of the most eloquent anti-human rights advocates of the left ultimately argue that rights and freedoms are merely an historic and now out-of-date attempt at cloaking unfettered free markets in a higher morality. Their shield theory is the polar opposite of the Trojan horse analysis of their fellow sceptic – if Conservative – cousins.

One source of the argument is the apparent primacy of civil liberties, including the peaceful enjoyment of property and personal privacy (including over financial affairs), over social, economic and cultural rights to food, shelter, healthcare and so on. Another comes from historical analysis of rights arguments being deployed as a bulwark against and criticism of the Soviet Union, the People's Republic of China and other leftist attempts at government in Latin America and elsewhere. An often proffered example is the 1970s revisionist spin on 1960s American military adventures in Vietnam.[14]

For some, the championing of religious and media freedom has repeatedly been ripe for abuse by powerful vested interests against the vulnerable forces of progress, whether for women's dignity and reproductive rights, race equality or child protection. Recent attempts at refocusing the attentions of human rights defenders, international institutions and NGOs on social and economic rights are seen as merely the sad and cynical efforts by human rights lawyers to save their increasingly irrelevant and failing brand from obsolescence.[15]

Horses for Courses

The liberties of the wealthy have continually been prioritized over the needs of the poor. But the question is whether this necessarily flows from the human rights framework itself, or instead simply from the nature of greed and power on the planet. Is it right that legal and constitutional models of guaranteeing civil and political rights, in contrast with the progressive political realization of social, economic and cultural rights, creates a hierarchy of value?

I say no. Delivering fair trials in court and healthcare in hospitals does not make either service less important. Of course, some trials concern crimes, negligence or discrimination that took place in a healthcare context. However, in the first instance and for the most part, notwithstanding necessary legislation and regulation, cherished healthcare is delivered by medics and not lawyers. The same applies to education by teachers, homes by builders and food by farmers. In contrast with the delivery of essential but abstract civil liberties, the role of the law is secondary in relation to socio-economic rights.

Further, civil rights to peaceful enjoyment of property and private and family life belong as much to the poor as to the wealthy. If anything, the poor need these rights more than those who are sitting comfortably on established and largely unchallenged privilege in society. Without these rights, poorer people face the bullying of bailiffs, foreclosure, destitution and even imprisonment, without any legal process or protection. This used to happen all over the world, even for the smallest debts and at the whim of creditors. The poor are certainly more likely to face arbitrary home and body searches without proportionate levels of suspicion or protection. Such intrusive police power is much more rarely used across the globe in the context of 'white-collar crimes' and tax fraud.

Nonetheless, there is no doubt that in their extensive marketing and lobbying, the international law firms whose particular client group is super-wealthy individuals and corporations have been quick to employ privacy arguments to hide the off-shoring of wealth in particular.[16] These may never reach the arena, let alone the judgement, of a court. Still, the fact that they are able to dress up vested interests with legal arguments in exchange for correspondingly generous slices of the pie does not make them any more legally or morally credible.

It is essential to remember that rights to peaceful enjoyment of property and private and family life are heavily *qualified* rights. They discipline the justification for and operation of public policy. They do not constrain its progressive development. Article 1 of the First Protocol to the ECHR is a good example in providing that:

> Every natural or legal person is entitled to the peaceful enjoyment of his possessions. No one shall be deprived of his possessions except in the public interest and subject to the conditions provided by law and by the general principles of international law.
>
> The preceding provisions *shall not, however, in any way impair the right of a State to enforce such laws as it deems necessary to control the use of property in accordance with the general interest or to secure the payment of taxes or other contributions or penalties.*[17]

It is hard to imagine a stronger or clearer assertion of the community's economic interests as that provided by the second paragraph of the Article. Arguably, this is not a qualification on property rights at all. This has already been provided by the public interest, legal conditions and international law tests in the first paragraph. Instead, it might be seen as a completely distinct and explicit assertion that, while property deprivation should not be arbitrary, discriminatory or corrupt – as is the case in so many lawless regimes throughout history and the world – active redistribution is without doubt a legitimate option for democratic societies.

The extension of property rights to 'legal persons' alongside natural ones in the Council of Europe and most of the world, sceptics argue, is itself a regressive measure, granting what should be a 'human' right to a company or corporation designed to protect economic advantage rather than human dignity. To me, this observation suggests important but insufficient reflection.

Firstly, the explicit reference to legal persons in this Article is in contrast with its absence in most other provisions of the Convention. This implies that a great many of these other protections simply cannot apply, except to 'real human beings'. Indeed, it would be nonsense to apply protections from torture, slavery, arbitrary detention and, I would argue, even self-incrimination to a non-living and non-breathing person. Save metaphorically, an organization cannot bleed, and in exchange for statutory benefits of incorporation, its members and investors should accept a degree of transparency and regulation that may include candour on the part of employees and directors.

However, if humans are to have rights to associate and to enjoy their property peacefully, part of that enjoyment must include the ability to form collective entities. These include trade unions, political parties, charities, banks and other companies (for and not for profit). If these may have their assets taken without law, whether by other private parties or by the state, the rights of millions of natural persons will be meaningless. It isn't just the members or investors sitting behind these corporate structures that would be deprived, but countless other employees, pension holders, creditors and potentially anyone who benefits from their goods and services.[18]

Left Field

Sceptics might further argue that, far from being the human rights *option* that I suggest, the conscious and constant greater levelling of wealth should be a positive duty upon all progressive and cohesive societies. As a matter of politics, I happen completely to agree. However, as a matter of *human rights* ethics, morals and law, this duty is limited to such redistribution as is required for the delivery of the various civil, political, social, economic and cultural rights that flow from the foundation of dignity. It is also significant that these were agreed by most nations of the world and the populations they represent, less than a century ago. To go further by stealth, as opposed to open and consensual development, would be to strip progressive politics of its own moral and creative force, priorities and choices.

To place too much of the burden of achieving greater economic parity – as opposed to non-discrimination – on a higher law rather than principled politics could actually slow or limit that aspiration. Compare a necessarily cautious judge's *interpretative* and safeguarding role with that of a politician armed with an *explicit* and immediate electoral mandate for radical redistributive change. Alternatively, it would render precious fundamental rights and freedoms the very anti-democratic Trojan horse that some right-wing thinkers accuse us of building and therefore feel justified in seeking to dismantle. Either way, this would be fool's gold for anyone who cares about the human race in turbulent times, and the poorest and most marginalized in particular.

As for the weaponization of human rights arguments against the former Soviet Union, China and other purportedly leftist governments by successive US governments in particular, one needs to separate intentional ideological competition and even periodic hypocrisy from the veracity of so many gross violations worldwide. Progressives do the cause of greater equality no favours by turning a blind eye to torture, slavery, censorship and death inflicted by self-styled people's governments of the left. Similarly, when the defenders of vast wealth inequality paper over the human rights abuses of their friends and allies, they merely hasten the end of their particular empires of the moment.

In Rights We Trust?

Religious and media freedoms are a difficult issue for many, not least as they increasingly seem to personify the interests of international and non-governmental empires rather than vulnerable individual consciences and voices.

We have already discussed the much-contested anti-abortion impact of the church on the American Charter in particular. I have expressed my own doubts about the arguably anachronistic 'protection of morals' justification for interference with freedoms of expression and association in the European Convention. However, the historic involvement and preoccupations of inevitably patriarchal organized religion cannot negate the whole human rights framework, any more than they devalue some of the most beautiful art and music ever devised as a result of religious inspiration and patronage.

Secular states have proved as capable of discrimination, oppression and cruelty as theocracies. Freedom of thought, conscience and religion is expressly freedom 'from' as well as 'to'. Consider religious dissidents throughout history. Think of Protestants, Catholics, women, and nonconformists in England long ago. Remember all Christians under Stalin, Muslims and others in today's China, and women and queer people in many parts of the Muslim world and beyond.

Nonetheless, some of the most significant dilemmas concern the fault lines between equal treatment, private and family rights on the one hand, and freedoms of association, conscience and religion on the other. As the secular world has been swifter to embrace various forms of equality, where does that leave religious rights to disagree and maintain communities based on that entrenched and sacred ideological difference?

No church or other faith community can be a no-go zone from the reach of human rights, without the kind of historic abuses that we have seen against women and children in particular potentially taking place. But pure faith and conscience, however misplaced, as opposed to their manifestation, must surely be absolute.

You must have the right to believe that I, as a woman, or even a woman of different faith or race, can never be your moral or intellectual equal. I would argue that you should even have the right to say so, subject to not inciting violence or putting me in fear. I would say that you should have the right to exclude me from your faith community or its hierarchy. This kind of freedom must include the right to be wrong.

However, once you enter the public realm as an individual or group, once you offer non-religious services and employments, whether in health, education or housing, etc., that manifestation of your faith must be subject to reasonable limits by the law of the land. This law must include the core human rights value of non-discrimination.

Media freedom can be similarly hard to defend when global communications barons have elected national leaders at their beck and call and elections seemingly in their gift. In some parts of the world, these less than accountable relationships may shift the balance of power in the other direction. In any event, the super-wealthy and powerful, like other less-palatable poster children for rights, may be accused of 'abusing' hard-won freedoms in order to evade scrutiny and justice. Still, to make a spurious and ultimately unsuccessful moral or legal argument must surely to some extent itself be a fundamental right. It is incumbent on democratic society and those who govern or defend it to counter with the reasons why such spurious arguments should not succeed.

The absolute right against inhuman and degrading treatment should always trump the qualified rights to enjoyment of property and privacy engaged by 'non-disclosure agreements' and 'super-injunctions'. These controversial instruments work against the public interest to cover up abuse by perpetrators who simultaneously argue *against* human rights in general, and private and family life in particular – for mere mortals rather than themselves. However, as discussed above, spurious privacy arguments do not mean that privacy has no value.

It may have been easier to argue for an absolute right to free speech in the world of quill pens and even during the age of the printing press, when the powerful ruled by decree. In those times, the very acts of writing and publication seemed almost inherent exercises in dissent. This may to some extent explain the more qualified framing of freedom of expression in post-war conventions and constitutions, compared with the 1791 US Bill of Rights. That said, even Article 11 of the French Declaration of 1789 created an arguably circular and open-ended exception for:

> what is tantamount to the abuse of this liberty in the cases determined by law.

In any event, after the subsequent advents first of broadcasting and then the internet, technological developments that once seemed cause for unadulterated celebration have yielded rather more complex results for human flourishing.

The airwaves were used for and against fascist propaganda before and during World War II. In Rwanda in the 1990s, they once more became a tool for inciting genocide.[19] Today, new media platforms may be a means of either democratic empowerment or totalitarian oppression. Ours is an age of less than transparent borders between corporations and states and blurred lines between online truth and illusion. This new frontier of human rights is both a challenge and an opportunity. However, one thing seems clear. While the technology and its commodification have moved at pace, the ethics, governance, politics and law have woefully lagged behind. This would seem self-evidently to be a case of the underdevelopment of human rights practice, not its excess.

In the meantime, wholesale sceptics of right and left will whine at every attempt to thwart their worst authoritarian and discriminatory instincts. They cry foul when the abuses of their flagship regimes are weaponized by opponents to undermine even the nobler ideals of their politics. Still, the abuses were, and continue to be, real in the first place. As long as that is the case and the risk, the framework of universal protections must be defended. However, for human rights folk, still thornier questions arise in the negotiation and application of competing freedoms.

4.
When Rights Clash

I shall never get you put together entirely.
Pieced, glued, and properly jointed.

Sylvia Plath[1]

Inevitably, sometimes in reality or more often in perception, rights will clash. Far from being a failure in the framework, this is perhaps one of the best tests of its resilience. We see such claimed clashes at every level of society, from the fractured family to the United Nations. However, when considering these, as with every other area of human rights application, a little calm, dispassionate and logical discipline can be of huge help.

Phoney Wars

At the outset we must realize that many so-called clashes of rights, whether referred to in politics or the media, are not really conflicts between human rights claims at all. Really they are slightly sloppy, colloquial and hackneyed references to people's competing ambitions and interests. We are often told that liberty for the wolf, fox, pike or other predatory creature will be less than attractive to the sheep, hen or minnow. However, this notion of unfettered freedom, including being at liberty to kill, is simply not a human rights value at all, let alone a concept reflected in any legal document.

Having created this straw man in a state of nature, unconstrained by the 'democratic society' constantly referred to in human rights laws, some commentators then swoop in with the notion of his rights being forfeited by any number of graphic examples of heinous behaviour.[2]

However, in post-war human rights thinking, the murderer who is sentenced to imprisonment in truth faces neither forfeiture of their rights nor even a conflict with them. There being no 'forfeiture', as opposed to qualification, is extremely important. Even the convicted prisoner has vital rights not to be tortured and degraded, to access to lawyers and appeals and so on. In this particular example, and as we have already seen, the 'right to liberty' is actually only protection from *arbitrary detention*. Incarceration following a *lawful sentence* expressly does not conflict with this carefully defined right. This is true even for lesser offences than murder, and when some of us penal reformers would strenuously argue that a non-custodial penalty would have adequately, or much better than prison, met the aims of the justice system.

Similarly, some human rights sceptics set up zero-sum games between, say, liberty and security, or privacy and expression, in the abstract. They either deliberately or innocently ignore the fact that, successfully or otherwise, the drafters of the principal post-war international and domestic human rights declarations, charters, conventions and constitutions have attempted to include all of these sometimes competing but often complementary values. They have done this in a manner that allows them to be weighed, balanced and applied in practice. They anticipated 'hard cases' into which their generation had significant, if not quite superhuman, insight.

The right to liberty or against arbitrary detention may be described as a 'procedural' right. However, in the areas of 'qualified' or 'balanced' rights too, there are a whole range of daily, necessary, proportionate and lawful 'interferences'. These simply do not amount to a rights conflict, still less a violation. Not to acknowledge this is to undermine severely the robustness of centuries of human rights evolution leading up to the post-war settlement itself.

Let's say that I am the member of a radical movement which the intelligence agencies believe to have engaged in attempts to undermine parliamentary democracy. I have been subject to various forms of intrusive surveillance, to the banning of my organization, seizure of my assets and, following criminal conviction, imprisonment for a protest-related offence, and electoral disenfranchisement.

In the context of my privacy, conscience, speech, association, property and voting rights, I might argue that a particular intrusion or restriction that the state has imposed upon me fails to fall within one of the justifications for interference. I might further argue that the decision in question is disproportionate to the aim pursued, or that the law employed is insufficiently clear. In rebuttal, the authorities will argue that they or the relevant legislators by whom they are empowered are defending various vital interests of society, as anticipated by human rights laws. These justifications may well include 'the rights and freedoms of others'.

One side or the other will for the moment ultimately prevail. I will be found to have had my rights seriously violated or, alternatively, merely lawfully and proportionately limited.

However, this rather routine type of human rights exercise is not very accurately or helpfully described as a 'conflict' or 'clash' of rights.

Campus Wars

Many of the heated rows and 'culture wars' that have blown up on university campuses in recent years – over speakers with controversial views being disinvited or protested against – fall into this category of phoney wars. 'Clashes of rights' in this context are often merely inevitable clashes of substantive opinions, ideas and even values, rather than a genuine clash of one person's freedom of expression with the competing right of another. There is no 'right not to be offended'.

If at times students, academics or others have been censored or intimidated, that may be a straightforward violation of their right to freedom of expression. If certain universities favour some groups and views and suppress others, there may be discrimination, subject to their prerogative to foster evidence-based research and academic rigour.

Complications are added by wider academic freedom and freedom of association, which encompasses both free and rigorous inquiry and rights both to associate with *and disassociate from* others. These principles should make any democratic state slow to intrude too much into the academy, and academic governance slow to intrude into student unions and other self-governing bodies. Here the members should have some reasonable latitude, so as to experiment with rubbing along together. However, to be disagreed with and even sometimes heckled is not the same as being silenced. The best way of promoting free speech is by tolerating the disagreeable speech of others, not by competing for victimhood every time disagreement becomes too loud.

War or Other Public Emergency

In his fascinating book *On Human Rights*[3] the late moral philosopher James Griffin gives the example of internment policies and the suspension of *habeas corpus* on both sides of the Atlantic, during World War II and after 9/11, as a conflict of human rights. Under the professor's analysis, the conflict is between the rights of potentially wholly innocent suspects to be brought before a court within a reasonable time, and those of civilians who might lose their lives but for the internment of others.

With enormous respect and more than a little trepidation, at least as a matter of human rights *law*, I must disagree. The metaphysics of separating innocent from potentially guilty suspects is unnecessary. Both have the procedural right not to be detained indefinitely without charge. Indeed, this right is designed fairly to allow us to distinguish the innocent from the guilty. In legal terms, it is similarly unnecessary to crystallize a contrasting hypothetical group of civilians protected by the policy. The state's obligation to protect life (though inevitably not absolute) is not limited to civilians, and would, in a better human rights analysis of Griffin's scenario, even extend both to the unfortunate innocent and any guilty detainees.

We have already considered emergency exception or derogation provisions in, for example, the International Covenant on Civil and Political Rights and the ECHR. In my view, they rightly exist for moments of such grave and overwhelming emergency that the rule of law, systems of justice and rigorous rights protections simply may not operate in the usual way.

The Government, in the first instance, though no doubt subject to judicial scrutiny thereafter, must decide whether such a state of emergency truly exists and whether the rights-suspending measures it proposes are strictly necessary and in keeping with international law.

These thresholds are obviously far higher than those that apply every day, when states interfere with qualified rights to, say, privacy or property enjoyment in order to protect their populations from harm. It is important to remember that the right to life in peacetime and protections from torture, degradation, slavery and retrospective punishment may not be derogated from. In the final analysis, contemporary courts and subsequent scholars will decide and reflect on whether the thresholds were actually met. Was there really a true emergency? Was the internment strictly necessary and therefore lawful under the circumstances?

However, emergency internment policies and other derogations are not about two real and distinct groups of rights holders pleading with the authorities for their particular claims to prevail in a conflict. They are, for these purposes, merely the most dramatic example of governments being expressly allowed to limit, in this case even temporarily suspend, some individual rights in the wider public interest. At no point do they involve a forensic evaluation of whether the rights to life or liberty must prevail in a particular direct clash.

Human versus Other Rights

Sometimes a conflict will be said to occur between human and more 'ordinary' kinds of legal rights. Perhaps the authorities in a particular city are considering whether to continue with an experimental road scheme. In this pilot, cyclists have been able to ride on walkways previously reserved for pedestrians. The trial of the policy has been hotly contested.

Cyclists celebrate how much easier it has been for them to get around safely and easily, unimpeded by dangerous and often grid-locked road traffic. Groups representing the elderly and people with disabilities point to their increased fear of using the walk-ways and a moderate but significant rise in accidents affecting the vulnerable in particular. Parents' groups are split, roughly according to the age of their children. Those with teenagers would rather they cycled on the pavements, while those with infants in prams or younger children on foot would prefer that these returned to being bike-free. Motorists have been glad to have the roads to themselves, and environmentalists believe that there should be more pedestrianized areas and cycle paths instead.

This kind of public policy debate engages millions of people in their various communities every day. We may not and perhaps should not see it primarily through the lens of human rights as opposed to a question of many other competing considerations. It would be hard for cyclists sensibly to suggest that they have a fundamental human right to the footpath or for pedestrians to argue for a right to walkways that are completely wheel-free, certainly not from electric wheelchairs and other mobility vehicles.

However, the one potentially obvious human right in play, alongside whatever ordinary legal rights have for the moment been allocated by the political community, is the right not to be discriminated against in the context of other rights and freedoms. If the pilot scheme *did* demonstrate a disproportionate and dangerous impact on the very young, old or differently abled, a human rights-respecting local authority would take that very seriously when deciding what to do next.

But what if the ten additional deaths and 100 serious cycle injuries caused to vulnerable pedestrians on the walkways during the period of the pilot were countered by an identical reduction in equivalent injuries to cyclists on the roads? What if the reduction in cyclists' injuries was even greater than those sustained by vulnerable pedestrians during the trial? Would that evidence explode the human rights argument against the scheme being continued in its current form, without at least some additional restraints on cyclists' use of the footpaths? I would say not.

Firstly, while proportionality is one hurdle for a lawful interference with a classic qualified right such as privacy or freedom of expression, this is never a straightforward numbers game of comparing how many people win or lose from a particular policy. In the human rights stakes, dignity trumps even utility. It is vital to gauge the gravity of the harm to the few, even against the benefit or mitigation of harm to the many.

Secondly, those deploying the greater previous number of cycle deaths in an attempt to trump the rights of vulnerable pedestrians cannot sensibly argue that these deaths could not have been addressed by any number of alternative policies that did not sacrifice the rights of pedestrians to walk down the street in relative safety.

Thirdly, to ride a bicycle, drive a car or use any new or future form of transport of our devising is a privilege that may attract 'legal rights' in certain circumstances and under certain constraints. To walk safely outside one's front door is more obviously associated with the right to life, to private and family life and autonomy, to free association and so on. When discrimination is in play, the offending act or omission need not actually have violated the principal rights themselves.

Discrimination need only put its toe on their territory, the ball merely clip the white line.

Finally, and as already discussed, in the realm of human rights, discrimination is special. So much so, that apparently trivial slights, like being refused a table in a café or being asked to sit at the back of a bus, become grave and infamous abuses when targeted at certain groups. Indeed, while there is room for all sorts of debate about what is or is not truly discriminatory, whether directly or indirectly, to allow the rights of the minority group and especially one defined by immutable characteristics (such as childhood or old age or infirmity) to be totally sacrificed for the benefit of the majority would drive a coach and horses, rather than ride a mere bicycle, through the protection of human dignity.

As is so particularly apparent in health, security and other emergencies in particular, it is this principle more than any other that distinguishes human rights folk from the libertarians with whom they will sometimes make common cause, but rarely be in harmony. Many self-styled libertarians will seek minimal restraints, even at the expense of the vulnerable. If restraints, intrusions or even inconvenience for the many might be avoided by singling out a particular group, this will seem logical and desirable to them.

They are the voices for overt racial profiling at the airport, and isolating the elderly during epidemics and pandemics to allow a virus to rip through the majority population in pursuit of 'herd immunity'. Human rights defenders will subject restraints on fundamental freedoms to extremely rigorous and structured scrutiny. However, for them, the greatest sin is to sacrifice the vulnerable. That is their *immunity from the mentality of the herd*. As in hundreds of war films, and even as the bullets fly, they will not leave anyone behind.

Absolute versus Other Human Rights

If human dignity is a core value that expands into many and various forms of our flourishing, the rights that protect it can also be seen as a series of concentric circles. We have already discussed the variety of ways in which human rights have been framed, and the very few that might in any way be described as absolute. Nonetheless, rights against torture, inhuman and degrading treatment and slavery are just that. So what happens when they are pitted against other procedural or qualified fundamental human rights?

While torture, inhuman and degrading treatment and slavery are distinct concepts, they all go to the heart of the gravest violations of human dignity. This is the individual human just trying to survive in the face of grinding oppression, even before attempting the various social interactions that are inherently human and are accordingly recognized in all the other rights and freedoms.

Before I reignite a debate about any alleged primacy of civil and political over social and economic rights, and notwithstanding the different enforcement mechanisms for these categories, it is worth remembering that, in extreme examples, for the state to deprive a human of the basic means of existence will constitute one of these absolute violations. It may become a form of inhuman and degrading treatment. Even in my own country, the UK, where social and economic rights have not to date been constitutionalized in the same way as civil and political ones, this has been the thinking of the highest courts in the context of the forced destitution of asylum seekers as a tool of government policy to make them unwelcome, and so deter further arrivals.[4]

With a human rights rationale worthy of Lord Mansfield in *Somerset's Case*, the late and ever-humane Lord Brown of Eaton-under-Heywood had advanced such thinking while still in the Court of Appeal, and even two years before the UK's Human Rights Act expressly armed UK judges with Convention rights in 1998:

> Parliament cannot have intended a significant number of genuine asylum seekers to be impaled on the horns of so intolerable a dilemma: the need either to abandon their claims to refugee status or alternatively to maintain them as best they can but in a state of utter destitution.[5]

Rape Trials

We have already considered the genuine clash of the right against inhuman and degrading treatment with the fair trial right to defend yourself, in person, in a rape trial. In the face of this clash between an absolute and a procedural human right, the then European Commission on Human Rights found in favour of rape complainants not being cross-examined by their alleged perpetrators, unmediated by counsel. US courts have taken a similar approach to this clash of rights. Subsequent legal and political opinion seems to have agreed, or at least acquiesced, not least perhaps when fair trial violations are more often, and likely, caused by not having access to lawyers rather than being *required* to have them in certain grave and exceptional circumstances.

Nonetheless, investigations and trials for the gravest crimes, and perhaps for sex crimes in particular, may pose further and less easily resolved conflicts. On the one hand there are the absolute rights of complainants and of potential victims not to be degraded and to have protection from abusers. On the other hand, the consequences of being wrongly publicly suspected, let alone convicted, of this kind of crime are so life-shattering as to warrant pre-charge protections, the most rigorous standards of due process and the strong presumption of innocence for the accused.

This clash of rights is further complicated by social attitudes around sexual mores and consent. These are often highly contested and subject to a great deal of local, let alone international, variation over time. To those who believe that the number of previous sexual intimates a person has had makes them more or less likely to have consented on the occasion of an alleged rape, this line of questioning seems perfectly relevant and reasonable.

Mercifully, there are now many jurisdictions where this kind of cross-examination as to sexual history has been tightly limited for fear of degrading or undermining a complainant to no genuine probative value.

However, even within these legal systems, there will be the cases where a complainant's evidence of particular sexual or violent acts 'that they would never have consented to' must give rise to a right of rebuttal. If this extends to combing through years of a complainant's correspondence or social media posts, lengthy seizure of their mobile phone and other disproportionate treatment of dubious relevance, these trials will be such an ordeal for complainants that few will come forward. To effectively decriminalize such grave crimes in practice is an abject human rights failure in any civilized society.

However, when an absolute right clashes with an obviously qualified one, the former must succeed. This phenomenon is most commonly and graphically demonstrated within families.

The family in all its developing incarnations is essential to humanity. It is jealously protected by human rights doctrine. The right to respect for private and family life has been an important shield against undue interference by various states with the most intimate relationships of various kinds (including same-sex and transnational partnerships). This is so much the case that many sceptics are wary of this right in particular.

However, when those precious relationships become dangerous, to the extent that the vulnerable are exposed to the gravest abuses of power in the home, the conflict of rights between respect for the family and protection from inhuman and degrading treatment has been resolved with relative ease. In the European Convention jurisdiction at least, prohibiting the absolute violations of individual humans that were 'corporal punishment' of children[6] and rape within marriage[7] roundly trumped even respect for the institution that is the family.

Clashes of Qualified Human Rights

So far, so relatively straightforward. Human rights should trump other legal rights in any constitutional democracy that has made adequate provision for fundamental freedoms as enshrined in international law. Protection of the relatively few rights that are absolute will be the clearest of all justifications for proportionate interference with a qualified right such as private or family life, whether in the case of a domestic search warrant, telephone tap or prosecution for child cruelty or marital rape. Procedural fair trial rights may pose more of a challenge when weighed against the absolute rights of complainants, but with expertise, investment and careful judicial control many of these tensions may be eased.

What about a clash between two obviously qualified rights, each allowing for justified proportionate interference? Ironically perhaps, given that the structure of these rights grants the most latitude for democratic decision-makers, this kind of conflict may be among the hardest for legislators, officials and courts to resolve.

Privacy versus Expression

Obvious and high-profile cases arise when one person's free expression interferes with another's private and family life. A great deal is made of the slightly differing constitutional and cultural attitudes to this clash around the world. While much-publicized litigation between tabloid news giants and celebrities may not seem like the coal face of human rights practice, the underlying values and arguments will be increasingly important, if we as an international community are ever properly to bring the rule of law to the Wild West of the internet, just as it was once imposed (if exploitatively) by former empires on 'newly discovered' continents and (perhaps more benignly) on the high seas.

Famously, and while the US First Amendment is not quite as absolute as it might seem, it contains an explicit right to free speech in contrast with more apparently limited privacy rights that have to be implied when reading the Bill of Rights.[8] By contrast, Articles 8 and 10 of the European Convention are cast in very similar and qualified terms with neither obviously nor automatically trumping the other.

While all developed jurisdictions respect speech and privacy values and are grappling with many of the same challenges in the modern world, the rights nationalists in the British media, in particular, look enviously across the Atlantic, even while scowling over the English Channel towards mainland Europe with its dreaded Churchillian Human Rights Convention. What the great man would have made of twenty-first-century-style intrusions into his own private life is an interesting thought experiment, given his own journalism on the one hand and occasional disputes with parts of the press on the other.

In an age of telephoto lenses, facial recognition technology, mobile devices, large volumes of digital, including biometric, information and the internet, it is important to understand that 'private life' exists even outside the home or office. It can protect places, activities and material over which there is a 'reasonable expectation of privacy'.[9] So, there might be an interference, even by way of images captured in a public street via CCTV or a press photographer. This has been found to apply to, for example, pictures of someone entering a place of drug rehabilitation,[10] or even where their suicide attempt in a public place was caught on camera and subsequently televised.[11]

While we can all imagine examples of inquiry into public figures' and even normally private people's personal lives being 'in the public interest', the precise parameters of even this justification are hard to set in stone.

As with even convicted prisoners, people cannot be said to have *forfeited* their rights to respect for private and family life, their home and correspondence altogether. So, notwithstanding the explicit and pressing counter-balance of expression rights of the media and the public, each specific intrusion will have to come within the lawful exceptions in Article 8.2. In the case of the *clash* with expression rights, this will likely and self-evidently be 'for the protection of the rights and freedoms of others'.

Illegality, hypocrisy or other wrongdoing are more likely to meet this test than other private activity or information. However, the identity of serious criminals may warrant protection for fear of vigilantism, violence and even death.[12]

Family members, especially children, of claimants bring their own rights to private life which may be harder, though not impossible, to justify intruding upon. The fact that material is already to some extent publicly available may dislodge its private nature, but not necessarily or completely. The nature and degree of any claimed likely harm that would be caused by publication will be relevant to the question of proportionality.

When the state has already legislated or provided codified guidance, domestic and international courts are likely to give this a fair degree of latitude in the form of judicial deference (domestically), or a margin of appreciation (internationally). Importantly, however, an international court such as the European Court of Human Rights will, almost by definition, be examining an alleged privacy or free expression violation *after the event*, in considering a claim by, say, an individual or media outlet against the state where it took place. A domestic court may also potentially be deciding on, for example, an alleged breach of confidence between two private parties after the event.

However, it may alternatively be deciding on whether to grant an injunction *preventing* the publication of allegedly private information. While sometimes undoubtedly justified, this is the most serious potential interference with the free expression rights of press, public and other private individuals. It will always be a matter of individualized case-by-case judgement.

In these extremely hard cases, a court will be forced to go

through the parallel discipline of judging whether the suppression of publication meets the tests set out by the qualifications to the free expression right delineated in Article 10.2. Where the putative publicity relates to a criminal conviction or civil judgement, the Article 6 rebuttable presumption in favour of public justice is also in play. This is almost the human rights equivalent of a complex simultaneous equation.

In practice, the claimed privacy rights of the party resisting publication and the expression rights of the would-be publisher will be weighed against each other with factors such as the timing and breadth of the potential disclosure or injunction. These will be added to the calculation alongside the potential consequences of granting or not granting the judicial relief. Here, and unlike in so many other human rights cases more generally, a court is deciding the scope of competing individual people's rights first hand, rather than second-guessing other public authorities' decisions and reasoning.

It is important to remember that this kind of dispute is not just about the lucrative game of cat and mouse between media empires and wealthy celebrities. In an age of mobile devices and social media platforms, the principles can just as easily be engaged by arguments between private individuals with each other. However, unlike the owners of tabloids and tiaras, they may lack the means to have these properly and fairly resolved.

Crucially, though, while it is so easy to think of privacy and expression rights in constant discord, there are also numerous and increasing occasions when they are completely aligned. A great deal of brave and risky expression, for example, by whistleblowers and other vulnerable people will always be easier to achieve under a cloak of anonymity. Hence the protection of journalistic sources and communications encryption are as much a matter of the right to free expression as to privacy. This has been acknowledged by the European Court of Human Rights,[13] the African Commission on Human and Peoples' Rights[14] and the Inter-American Declaration of Principles on Freedom of Expression.

Protest versus Property

In turbulent times, domestic courts are likely to be faced with more and more dilemmas about the proportionate and lawful interference with peaceful protest rights to association, assembly and expression. Where the state has stepped in, for example by way of police powers and criminal offences, even if acting notionally on behalf of property owners and other businesses, this isn't really a genuine clash of rights at all. The state is not the bearer of these property rights, so the courts will merely be second-guessing whether it has taken justified, lawful and proportionate action under the qualifications to the various rights involved in peaceful dissent.

The more classic clash, as with privacy and expression cases, arises where the courts are asked by private property-holders themselves to protect their peaceful enjoyment by way of injunctions and other orders prohibiting or removing the protests of particular people or groups, or in particular places at particular times. In mature democracies, this will often involve re-examining traditional causes of action such as 'nuisance', in the light of countervailing human rights to protest. This is complicated by the increasing private ownership of apparently public space, and is likely to involve constant, messy but essential compromise, rather than perfect legal formulae.

This type of rights cacophony may be more improvised jazz

than symphonic arrangement. Still, when well judged, it is the fine art of safeguarding freedom.

Faith versus Equal Treatment

Other genuine and often high-profile clashes of rights arise where the tectonic plates of freedom of thought, conscience and religion and equal treatment collide. This is not the glamorous world of Hollywood or the cloak-and-dagger one of National Security. In the common or garden workplaces of bakers, bureaucrats, hoteliers and health professionals, a number of the most contested conflicts occur, sometimes even leading to litigation in the highest courts.

Freedom of thought, conscience and religion is absolute. Its *manifestation* is qualified. For obvious historical and philosophical reasons, equal treatment is at the heart of post-war human rights protection. Clear tensions exist in the context of a range of day-to-day employments and services, where the faith or conscience of the service-giver and the nature of the service, or identity of the service-user, are at odds. Many of these tensions will be eased or avoided by employers finding pragmatic solutions, not unlike the *reasonable adjustments* they make so as not to discriminate against various groups of workers. However, this will sometimes be difficult, undesirable or impossible.

We have already discussed how women's reproductive rights (inherent in rights to dignity, privacy and bodily autonomy) have long clashed with the deeply held religious convictions of many people. To be fair, all societies must constantly grapple with thorny questions of when rights-bearing human life begins and ends in any viable sense. National and regional systems have taken dramatically different approaches to this problem. In some jurisdictions, the political and legislative compromise has been to allow relevant health professionals a form of conscientious objection to giving some kinds of treatment. Even this has led to a number of specific disputes in practice.

Other clashes arise when the conscience of a specific worker, business or religious group conflicts with the rights to equal treatment of people of different faiths, races, sexes or sexualities. This area of international comparative human rights conflict resolution could fill a large tome in itself. I will simply suggest some examples alongside the type of approach to resolving them that I believe most consistent with the underlying values at stake.

The Case of the Marriage Registrar

The international framework explicitly recognizes the rights of adults to marry. This is also implicit in the right to respect for private and family life. However, it is highly caveated with a large discretion accorded to individual states (and in some of them, even subject to local variation) to legislate the precise rules about the age, sex and other status of the parties.

What if a state legislates to allow same-sex marriage and one of its registrars deeply disapproves on account of their religious beliefs or other firmly held convictions? Should the employer be required by human rights principles and laws to accommodate this objection? Should the employee be able to refuse to register same-sex marriages and a system be devised to ensure that this can always happen in a timely and sensitive manner, so as not to discriminate against these couples?

The hardest cases would seem to arise during moments of

transition, where a long-time employee is faced with a whole new cultural and, crucially, legal settlement. In these cases, there is a strong proportionality argument for giving the employee at least a period of time during which they may officiate in some cases and not others.

However, even this must be subject to the reasonable ability or otherwise of the authority to devise a system for this accommodation that does not risk placing an undue burden on other employees, or, worse still, subjecting the same-sex couples to discrimination and humiliation. All new registrars must be expected to sign up to administer the law of the land, and in due course even existing staff who cannot reconcile this with their beliefs can reasonably be expected to find alternative employment. They are not conscripts in an army, entitled conscientiously to object to fighting and accordingly assigned to other duties. Pacifists need not enlist in a volunteer army and religious objectors should not apply for jobs administering services to which they violently object.

The Case of the Heretic Cleric

Faith communities around the world have moved in different ways and at different speeds to accommodate the rights of women and minorities, and theological differences within their own denominations. Some have moved dramatically, and others barely at all. In some countries, periods of liberalization of doctrine and practice have been followed by regression in the rights of women and dissident groups.

What if a religious tradition refuses to ordain women, to marry people of the same sex, or even to allow into their congregation people with less than completely orthodox views? Should that faith group be required, under threat of legal sanction, to respect the rights of everyone to participate fully within it?

To me, this is almost the mirror of the previous example. Democratic society must be able to evolve, in order better to embrace the core human rights value of equal treatment. It must be able to administer the laws of the land. However, for freedoms of faith, conscience and association to mean anything, they must include a certain irreducible room for resistance to this wider societal consensus.

Whatever the best ethical or theological path, religious freedom must include the right *not* to ordain women, LGBTQ+ people or those whose views are too beyond the consensus of the specific community. This must further include discriminatory and exclusionary principles for the congregation; a right to be wrong. However, there will be other areas of the life of this tight-knit community where it is justified, proportionate and even essential to interfere.

The education and welfare of children is an obvious example. Even faith schools can be expected to abide by minimum standards as to the curriculum and regime. As we have seen in the context of other clashes of rights, children are not the mere chattels of their parents. Adoption and other children's services are another example, as may be a host of other services and employments available to the wider public. Surely there is no principled reason why a faith community should be allowed to discriminate in its employment of gardeners or provision of food to the hungry? States must have a significant degree of latitude in regulating these areas of faith-based and other social action in the wider community.

No Room at the Inn

This brings me further outside the religious institution, hierarchy or community itself, to instances of businesses run by people of strong faith or other conviction militating, for example, against same-sex relationships. These may range from tiny family-run bed and breakfast lodgings to large corporate hotel groups. Some people think such disputes too trivial to really engage human rights at all. They fail to grasp the essential nature of the core value of equal treatment. It flows from the human dignity that is always violated when someone is discriminated against for who they are, and how they live their most intimate life. They should remember the origins of post-war human rights. They should reflect on Jim Crow and apartheid. Freedom of conscience is a precious right, but its manifestation is qualified by equally precious rights and freedoms.

Further confusion is created when the room that is on offer is little more than an extension of a person's or family's own dwelling. No reasonable state should compel me to take guests *per se*. Indeed, doing this is a classic hallmark of tyranny and would violate the right to respect for my home. However, a line can surely be drawn between offering hospitality to one's friends and family and offering services to the public *for a fee*. If I advertise a room for rent, even in my home, whether for the night or a more extended period, I must surely expect the arrangement to comply with the non-discrimination laws of the land.

Counselling, Protest and Prayer

Other potential clashes arise where people of faith seek to counsel, protest or pray for others, perhaps for their redemption or as to the 'error of their ways'. This will sometimes be at the individual, group or more institutional level, and covers activities from praying for your patients (whether they want this or not), offering conversion therapy and other questionable 'treatments', to protesting outside abortion clinics or other medical facilities.

The line between faith and modern medicine has been contested through time and all over the world. However, it is now well established that it is an area where the state is well placed to protect the vulnerable from abuses of power. So, while religious preaching and proselytizing must be respected alongside other free speech in a democratic society, so-called therapeutic intervention is ripe for state regulation, even where this offends certain faith-based sensitivities. The line may not always be an easy one to draw, but it must be attempted. All modern societies license the practice of medicine and there are a range of self-regulatory frameworks, transparency regimes and even legal prohibitions for non-medical therapies.

Both peaceful protest and public prayer are vital but nonetheless qualified human rights. When the target of a protest is a vulnerable individual rather than a government, commercial body or the public at large, proportionate interference with these rights may be easier to justify. The individual, say a woman entering an abortion facility, drug rehabilitation or gender identity clinic, has rights to privacy, including protection from harassment. These have to be weighed carefully in the prevailing local circumstances from time to time. As is so often the case, no one size, policy or law will fit all.

The Case of Dissenting Bakers

From time to time, an almost unexpected arena of conflict will appear and test our human rights thinking in a creative and ultimately perfectly positive way. It is easy to imagine issues of conscience around medicine and religion, and freedom of expression in the context of journalism. However, these may arise in other occupations as well.

In the light of earlier consideration of hotel services, it would be strange indeed if I thought purveyors of patisserie could discriminate on the grounds of sex, race or sexual orientation. However, what if the dispute is not about refusing to sell a cake to a person or couple, but refusing to ice a particular message on it?

As is so often the case, a lot turns on the best analysis of the essential nature of the dispute. To refuse to sell a birthday cake with a black or gay person's name iced on it looks like straightforward discrimination against a minority group and anathema to human rights. However, to refuse to ice a 'Black Lives Matter' or 'Pride' or 'Deeds not Words' campaigning slogan on a cake fits more easily into a rubric of freedom of conscience or expression.[15]

But what of a case where a baker refuses to ice the names of a same-sex or mixed-faith or -race (for that matter) couple on an anniversary cake? To my mind, this straightforward catering service is distinct from the political campaigning one where the baker is being asked to 'write' a specific slogan against their belief. It might as well be a marriage registration, hotel room or birthday cake. Democratic society having formed its consensus and laws on this issue, it would be odd if an individual's freedom of conscience could be deployed to frustrate this, by way of straightforward discrimination in the provision of goods or services.[16]

Social and Economic Rights

As discussed earlier, despite different international and domestic legal approaches to their delivery, there is no clear bright line or hierarchy between civil and political and social, economic and cultural rights. Rights to property, assembly and association (including by way of forming trade unions) and against forced labour are very explicitly civil rights. The right to strike is an expressly economic one. The right to education is very clearly included in both baskets, and in extreme cases to deprive someone of the social and economic rights to health, shelter, food, water and so on will breach the absolute civil right against degrading treatment.

Some national constitutions expressly recognize social, economic and cultural rights and even make them justiciable in local courts.[17] Others, potentially in combination with even older cultural and legal traditions or international law, create the possibility for some of these to be read into ostensibly civil and political rights in the context of pressing contemporary problems, such as water scarcity.[18]

There is inevitably a great deal of room for genuine conflict between the rights of various individuals and groups in these often highly contentious areas of public policy. This may include clashes between claims to competing social and economic rights and between civil and political ones. Subject to the jurisdiction where the clash arises or is being considered, these will have to be considered and, however temporarily and imperfectly, resolved on ethical, moral, political and even legal terms.

We have already discussed what I believe to be a mistaken view that civil and political rights are of a more precious order that will always trump social and economic ones. This is really a row about history, delivery and enforcement, rather than moral or practical priority. If anything, the fact that governments and electorates routinely prioritize their particular views of national economic well-being over individual civil liberties is what may require constitutional legal protection for the latter.

In any event, we have seen how state taxation is well within the justifications for lawful interference with property and forced destitution, capable of constituting degrading treatment. Globally (if regrettably in my view), the abolition of the death penalty has to a significant extent been left to progressive political realization. In this respect it has been treated not unlike inadequate healthcare, with even close cultural and political international allies such as the UK and the US politely agreeing to differ. So, it would seem that the relatively absolute or more qualified nature of rights may be more significant than their strictly civil or economic label.

Hence the qualified civil right to enjoy the proceeds of my property as a landlord may easily be proportionately interfered with by democratically imposed laws implementing my tenant's socio-economic rights to shelter, in the form of rent controls or eviction protections.

Where social and economic rights have been constitutionalized or simply legislated for, the courts may well have been designated a role in adjudication upon my fair employment or maternity rights, even though they clash with an employer's freedom of contract. Anyone who suggests that such rights were only ever a sop to the former Soviet Union and never intended to be made binding in the west might return to the third of Roosevelt's Four Freedoms: namely, from hunger.

Churchill's speech to the Conservative Party Conference in 1947 is also instructive:

> The trade unions are a long-established and essential part of our national life . . . we take our stand by these pillars of our British society as it has gradually developed and evolved itself, of the right of individual labouring men to adjust their wages and conditions by collective bargaining, including the right to strike . . .[19]

Over There, Over Here

Finally, on an ever-shrinking and interconnected planet, it is worth considering the direct clashes of rights between people in different parts of the world who are subject to vastly differential political, legal and wealth protections. When a multinational pharmaceutical, tech or energy giant, an international organization or a foreign power exploits local resources, labour or lawlessness, is the international system of human rights protection really able to do its job?

What, for example, is the responsibility or complicity of a state which actively seeks to profit from the incorporation of foreign or global companies via light-touch regulation, so that they might operate in other jurisdictions while escaping accountability under their laws and human rights norms? What are the human rights obligations of a mature democracy that trades, or permits its people to contract, with human rights-abusing states or companies overseas? This might be by purchasing the products of slave labour, providing police training or tools of surveillance, death and torture in those human rights-violating states.

Earlier on, I discussed the many phoney rights clashes that are really just occasions where national states may or may not be violating the human rights of some of their people in the name of a competing societal interest. But when those states are too small, weak or failed to perform or even attempt their most basic duties, genuine clashes of rights multiply. Even before that, we looked at the imperial–universal divide. Once, the mighty enriched themselves and abused their power via empires and colonies. They exceptionalized people and places so that rights were just for the chosen few. If today's global empires sail under logos instead of flags, surely any necessary human rights protections must adapt to police this new international piracy.

I have touched on the too-lawless virtual continent of the internet. Yet there still remain actual legal black holes – internment and refugee camps; human rights vacuums – exacerbated by climate conditions, territorial disputes and lengthy occupations.

There is also an increasing number of shadowy international trade and security agreements that appear to conflict with the fundamental rights and freedoms of ordinary people in favour of governments or corporations that do not even pretend to represent them.

Then, there is the question of unresolved historic abuse, including of the gravest kind. If there is rightly no 'statute of limitations' on vindicating human rights such as protection from torture, degradation, slavery and so on, what should we do about the continuing international and intergenerational legacy of those wrongs?

Universal human rights were always supposed, at least in part, to be a means of avoiding future civil and international wars. Nonetheless, as these wars continue to be waged, there are real questions about the responsibilities of the international community. If grave human rights abuses may sometimes justify even incursion into national sovereignty, is the United Nations, as currently structured, legitimate and competent for such a policing role? Some of these questions may be beyond reasonable resolution. To others, however, we must soon return.

5.
Modern Prometheus

I ought to be thy Adam, but I am rather the fallen angel . . .
Mary Wollstonecraft Shelley[1]

Mary Shelley never knew her pioneering mother Mary Wollstonecraft, who died shortly after bringing her into the world. Shelley would go on to leave a cultural legacy no less important, including writing the first science fiction novel, about Dr Frankenstein's misadventure in creating imperfect artificial life beyond his control. Shelley was writing in the early 1800s, at a time of accelerating industrial advancement and corresponding social upheaval. Then as now, many working people feared that new industries and automation would undermine their cherished skilled labour, livelihoods and lives.

The term 'Luddite' is now used pejoratively to describe ignorant and almost unthinking hostility to new technology. A fairer description of the original Luddites, some of whom physically attacked new industrial machines, is that they were concerned for workers' rights rather than implacably opposed to technology in itself. When Parliament introduced legislation to make what were their undoubted acts of criminal property damage a capital offence in 1812,[2] Mary Shelley's friend Lord Byron was one of the few who opposed it. His daughter Ada, Countess of Lovelace, would be a computing pioneer.

A series of Factory Acts in the 1800s and beyond led to the improvement of terms and conditions for industrial workers, including women and children. This included the ten-hour working day, improved ventilation, sanitation and machine safety in the industrial mills. A factory inspectorate was instructed to enforce the new rules. These protections were hard-won against the fierce objections of business owners and their political proxies. The contemporary task of taming global Big Tech, its investors and friends in high places is no less challenging and vital.

Buyer's Remorse

Despite the many benefits of our rich history of science and new technologies, occasional remorse will also feature in due time. The face of Albert Einstein is now the universally recognized icon of scientific genius. While his own work did not directly create the atomic bomb, his 1905 Special Theory of Relativity was revolutionary in revealing how a large amount of energy could be produced from a small amount of matter.[3] Like many other progressives and pacifists, his thoughts on war changed with the rise of Adolf Hitler. He fled his native Germany as a refugee in 1933, eventually landing in Princeton University in New Jersey. Third Reich external aggression and its splitting of the uranium atom in 1938 led some of Einstein's peers to fear the development of an atomic bomb by the worst possible custodians of such technology. So they enlisted the already world-renowned scientist to sign a 1939 letter to President Roosevelt,[4] one month before the invasion of Poland. This, and further letters in 1940, urged accelerated uranium research in the US.

Years later, not long before his death in 1954, reflecting upon how Roosevelt's successor President Truman had ended the Pacific War by dropping atom bombs on Hiroshima and Nagasaki, Einstein described his weapons development advocacy as the 'one great mistake of my life'.[5]

Of course, the scientists' conundrum was arguably far more nuanced than Truman's. Some feared the Nazis developing the A-bomb first. Truman deployed it in Japan even after Germany's defeat in order to shorten the war and avoid Soviet involvement on that seaboard. However, it is not just in the field of arms research that unrestrained scientific advances may present significant dangers to human well-being.

Biological and medical research and development can produce enormous ethical dilemmas around the beginning and end of life, and raise many complex issues around dignity, capacity and consent. It can morph into eugenics or work that produces grave health hazards and even devastating bioweapons. These may be rendered even more potent by our densely populated and interconnected contemporary world. Once more, the Covid-19 pandemic serves as a salutary warning.

A Space Odyssey

A new and arguably even more challenging human rights frontier has emerged in the world of computing, the internet, artificial intelligence (AI) and robotics. No doubt these combined technologies have brought some of the greatest opportunities for communication, creativity, ingenuity and learning since the invention of the printing press. Still, they present clear and present dangers to our rights not to be degraded, to fair process around important decisions, to privacy, expression, association, and against discrimination. They also create a number of practical challenges to the democratic model of government itself. Some experts and enthusiasts even predict or plan for a longer-term scenario where machines, benignly or otherwise, will create and populate the post-human future on this or other planets. Whether this last scenario seems plausible and fills you with excitement or dread, there are more pressing concerns.

In 2012, I had the privilege of participating in the opening ceremony of the Olympic Games in London. That occasion, seemingly celebrating a post-imperial progressive internationalism, now seems a very long time ago. A key moment involved Sir Tim Berners-Lee, the inventor of the World Wide Web, and his famous tweet: 'This is for everyone.'

Sixteen years earlier in Davos, American self-styled 'cyber-libertarian' John Perry Barlow penned and published 'A Declaration of the Independence of Cyberspace'.[6] It begins:

> Governments of the Industrial World, you weary giants of flesh and steel, I come from Cyberspace, the new home of Mind. On behalf of the future, I ask you of the past to leave us alone. You are not welcome among us. You have no sovereignty where we gather.
>
> We have no elected government, nor are we likely to have one, so I address you with no greater authority than that with which liberty itself always speaks. I declare the global social space we are building to be naturally independent of the tyrannies you seek to impose on us. You have no moral right to rule us, nor do you possess any methods of enforcement we have true reason to fear.

We have already considered the difference between unilateral 'declarations' and hard-negotiated 'conventions', and it would be completely unfair to sit in the armchair of hindsight, scoffing at the optimism, perhaps even naivety or arrogance of such statements. However, self-evidently, and notwithstanding its many gifts to human advancement, including for those who once lacked access to libraries and microphones, the online world is hardly 'independent' of tyranny.

We are constantly told that to be suspicious or even critical of new techno-empires is to be anti-technology and hostile to progress. Yet critical thinking is surely a prerequisite for a human rights approach far more in keeping with Berners-Lee's promise of genuinely being 'for everyone'.

'Inhuman' and Degrading Treatment

The right not to be subject to inhuman or degrading treatment is one of the few absolutes. Yet treatment contrary to this near-universally well-established maxim is, it seems, all but routine in cyberspace.

There are far too many examples of threats to kill and rape, as well as racialized and sexualized language and imagery of degradation that go largely unpunished online. Some of these amount to clear breaches of existing 'conventional' criminal law in most jurisdictions of the world. Many national police authorities lack the skills and resources to enforce the law online. Alternatively, they do not consider this to be a sufficient priority.

Social media platforms tend to enjoy greater legal protection than conventional media outlets and websites under the editorial control of news and entertainment companies.

Legislators, particularly in the US, have justified this approach on the basis of preserving both internet freedom for users and encouraging at least some modicum of responsible, pro-active and voluntary control by the companies themselves. The argument seems to be that if the internet is like a global town square, it should be policed by ordinary law enforcement rather than commercially risk-averse censorship. Alternatively, if the act of voluntarily removing harmful content automatically converted a social media platform into a publisher, these corporate giants might refrain from any ethical intervention whatsoever.

I have spent many years arguing with myself about what a human rights approach to regulating the internet would look like. One fundamental problem is with 'real world' analogies. The public square is supposed to be subject to the ordinary criminal 'laws of the land' (itself a problematic concept in a truly international space). However, the level of monopolistic control, monetization and potential for online harm suggests an environment perhaps more analogous with a licensed bar or cinema. These spaces have traditionally been subject to far greater state regulation, explicitly acknowledged by human rights instruments. We remember the way in which, for example, Article 10 of the ECHR made express provision for broadcast licensing in the early days of television after World War II.

This time around, the technology has moved at pace, in mostly private and corporate hands rather than public or democratically accountable ones. National governments and legislatures have been extremely slow to step in by way of international treaties or even purpose-specific domestic law. The online-as-offline equations for law enforcement have largely held sway.

This may be partly attributed to the technological naivety of senior policy makers and politicians, and partly to the sheer financial, communications and lobbying might of this giant industry dressed in the sheep's clothing of unfettered freedom. Whether the Californian 'tech bros' see themselves as explorers, pilgrims or settlers, they certainly don't feel instinctively bound by the mere laws of nations, even less so by the higher international human rights conventions pioneered in the mid-twentieth century.

But something clearly isn't working when reports of online child sexual grooming and real-time abuse, bullying – sometimes to the point of suicide – of vulnerable people and gross and degrading breaches of privacy have multiplied many times over in recent years.

This is before the even greyer area of algorithms that invite a vulnerable, or gambling- or pornography-addicted person into ever-darker echo chambers of content. This might be less harmful in an open environment where it would be subject to challenge and counter-propaganda, or in the case of a different person who isn't automatically being offered more and more of the same. Just as some of us might be directed towards historical fiction or music documentaries by our preferred book or film providers, anxious and depressed teenagers are being offered bespoke content relating to self-harm and suicide by greedy commercial platforms and advertisers, or just by malign fellow humans and bots.

The traditional childhood adage that 'sticks and stones will break your bones' contrasted with the harmlessness of mere communications rings increasingly hollow in a world where so many young people, in particular, live more and more of their lives physically atomized but socialized online. If the concept of brainwashing seems too infantilizing to its subjects, we must nonetheless at least begin to appreciate the huge potential for extreme influence.

Former sexual partners can publish intimate pictures and films taken with or without consent. They may do this with vengeance or enrichment in mind. The images may be uploaded and monetized with the capacity to go viral online. The consequences to the survivors, nearly all of whom are girls and women, are obviously extremely damaging for their personal, professional and social futures.

In the absence of genuine images, contemporary technology allows the creation of 'deepfakes'. These can of course include false and defamatory images and speech of political candidates and other public figures so as merely to lampoon them, or go much further and seriously undermine democracy. Entirely fabricated pornographic material, including featuring real people, may be commercially acquired and even made-to-order via websites easily accessible via the common search engines. Faces of a real person are transposed onto graphically sexual images of another's body. In some cases in the US, women have spent large sums of their own money paying lawyers to have the material taken down. Once more, any semblance of proactive self-regulation by the tech industry, let alone legislation and public law enforcement, lags woefully behind.

In all of these cases the architecture, use and profit model, combined with a governance deficit around this potentially wonderful and creative technology, is facilitating the inhuman and degrading treatment, and in some cases even torture and untimely death, of our fellow human beings. It is harming mental health, societal well-being and potentially even changing our brains and behaviour in ways we have yet fully to understand.

Kenyan staff sub-contracted to review internet content for feeding Californian AI products report the horrific consequences of constant subjection to depictions of violence, self-harm, murder, rape and child abuse. They are among the first to litigate against a neocolonial business model that renders poorly paid workers in the Global South the 'canaries in the coal mines' of this brave new world.[7]

Short of grave violations of such absolute protections, traditional due process rights to fairness and transparency in relation to a host of decisions of extreme importance to our lives are similarly under considerable threat. We see this in the context of, for example, education, employment, criminal justice, financial services and healthcare.

The End of Privacy?

It all begins with a transaction that we each make every time we engage with these exciting new technologies and give up a little more personal privacy. It develops into the 'surveillance state' and 'surveillance capitalism' models of China on the one hand, and the US and most of the rest of the world on the other. In exchange for apparently free or cheap access to the internet, we have turned ourselves, or at least a great deal of our private information and behaviour, into a commodity. Our data is then harvested, mined and sold on a breathtaking and ever-expanding scale. In recent years this data has come to include our internet searches, shopping, reading, entertainment and social media, as well as our physical home addresses, credit scores and even real-time geographical movements (via smartphones) and facial recognition.

In China every person who uses the internet must upload

their face for recognition, which becomes their virtual passport to a great many goods and services. The government is attempting to use its population's personal data to create a 'social credit system' of whitelisting and blacklisting people in an attempt to quantify trustworthiness.

Earlier this century, we watched western governments, law enforcement and intelligence services drift away from suspicion-based intrusions into an individual's personal privacy, towards the gathering and sifting of 'communications data' about entire populations in search of key words and patterns. This gave rise to many classic proportionality arguments about the balance between privacy and security.

However, in the 'free world' it is ultimately the corporations that are very much in charge. The EU has tried harder than most jurisdictions to make commercial data gathering and processing subject to consent, and rules limiting use to the purposes agreed to or otherwise legislated for in the public interest. Yet even this is limited protection in the face of the mountains of advertising and other incentives to 'click' and share one's information with various companies. Protection is more lax in the United States. We have yet to see where the UK will eventually settle on this spectrum in the longer term. In the turbulent years since Brexit, there have been many exorbitant promises of what a 'bonfire' of EU-derived protections, including data regulation, could offer to British commerce.[8] A similar 'light touch' is being suggested in relation to AI.[9]

One of the problems has been our ignorance about the technological capabilities as they have developed at speed. We have failed to understand the way that thousands of morsels of apparently uninteresting and 'not-so-private' information about our lives, interests, relationships and habits can build up a very intimate picture indeed. For many of us, a seizure of our mobile devices and trawl of the data and footprints they hold would be much more revealing than a search of our homes. The latter are still likely to be subject to far greater legal and physical protection.

When I first grappled with this subject in the early 2000s, I was concerned about the way in which authoritarian governments or serious organized criminals could use our private data against us. I did not predict the extent to which an equal or even greater threat might come from the Big Tech corporations that have now grown so greedy and complacent on our innocence and trust. Nor did I see past the more conventional privacy and discrimination violations that come with simply snooping on our lives. I did not imagine the even greater potential human rights challenges that come with combining huge amounts of personal data with algorithms, artificial intelligence and socio-economic power.

Civil, Criminal and the New Coded Code

To even attempt to understand how this new world might either improve or degrade the best human rights aspirations and protections of our existing one requires a reminder of what these really boil down to. To be effective, human rights must inform our ethics, morals and politics, and be to some extent expressed and delivered by enforceable law. Transparency and accountability are our allies in this project. But these same virtues are strenuously avoided by tech corporations. They are aided by commercial confidentiality and shareholder profit instead.

Laws and algorithms have a great deal in common: they

effectively comprise lists of instructions, which form decision-making trees. Laws are to be followed by people and 'legal persons' such as companies and governments. They are ultimately refereed by national and, in rare cases, international courts. As instructions, algorithms could in theory be applied by humans. Indeed, some of the best writers on the subject compare them to shopping lists, recipes or other well-understood human-to-human memos.[10]

Conversely, others describe law as 'social technology'.[11] However, in the current context, algorithms are more usually applied by computers with the capability to make calculations and decisions at high speed. Just as bad laws lead to injustice and even human rights violations, flawed algorithms will have the same result. The phrase 'garbage in, garbage out' comes from the early days of computing in the 1950s. It describes the dangers of feeding the machine corrupt or corrupted information. However, it could just as easily apply to laws, legal decisions or indeed social and economic systems built upon erroneous, discriminatory or 'inhuman' and degrading assumptions (such as racial and sexual supremacy) or false or mistaken facts.

In both cases, humans, with all their imperfections, draft the law or code with the obvious danger that harms become hard-wired in. Once embedded in the system, the injustice acquires an understandable, though undeserved, authority based upon the respected societal status of either legal or computerized code.

The War on Terror provided the most graphic examples of the oxymoron that is 'secret justice'. As we will see in the context of interrogation techniques in Iraq and elsewhere, this quickly became a curtain behind which even torture was perpetrated in freedom's name.[12] In that case, much if not all of the legal code was public and accordingly highly controversial. The administration of the law and policy was shielded from public scrutiny, but investigative journalists and public interest lawyers had at least some chance of being able to see the warning signs and take up the challenge. It is much more dangerous when the code itself, whether in the form of executive orders or computer algorithms, is shrouded in the secrecy of national security, commercial confidentiality, or both.

The transparency problem is acute enough in the case of conventional law, basic algorithms and artificial intelligence. However, *Advanced* AI or 'machine learning' only further compounds the problem. The computer isn't merely following the human-designed recipe any more. It is *teaching itself* to make decisions on the basis of vast amounts of data that it has devoured. What began as an academic experiment to see if a computer could beat a Grandmaster at chess[13] is now justified on the basis of corporate efficiency, profit and what is presented as an almost infallible 'magic' of the machine.[14] This is incomprehensible to most of us mere mortals, just as religion, economics and law have sometimes been deliberately mystified so as to disempower millions of people throughout human history.

The obvious danger is that existing injustices are multiplied inside the 'black boxes' of increasingly powerful corporations. We the people have neither the transparency nor the redress that human rights require. If we do not take fairly urgent democratic and legal action to ensure the enforcement of existing norms and laws and the development of new ones, we could be heading for a human rights 'ground zero'. This will be masked and powered by machines and their elite human masters greedy for profits and political power.

Centuries of local and global struggles for protection from

degradation and slavery, for privacy and fair trials could be significantly set back. So too, our social and economic rights to food, shelter, healthcare, education and work, without a major societal reset. Above all else, rights against discrimination, on grounds we have long believed to be unfair and which are at the heart of our human rights framework, could be undermined beyond recognition. This is why we must push back.

On 14 March 2023 (the eve of the 'Ides' for the classically superstitious), OpenAI, a company with major Microsoft investment, released its new AI system GPT-4. Within days, leading researchers claimed that the product demonstrated 'sparks of artificial general intelligence', or AGI, that matches the human mind across its full range of capabilities. By the end of the same month, an open letter organized by the MIT-led Future of Life Institute and signed by hundreds of prominent people in the field called for a moratorium on 'giant AI experiments'. Stuart Russell, a Computer Science professor at the University of Berkeley in California, was one of the signatories and explained his concerns as follows:

> It is in no country's interest for any country to develop and release AI systems we cannot control. Insisting on sensible precautions is not anti-industry. Chernobyl destroyed lives, but it also decimated the global nuclear industry. I'm an AI researcher. I do not want my field of research destroyed. Humanity has much to gain from AI, but also everything to lose.[15]

If this is beginning to sound a little alarmist, let me pause and try to explain.

In the pre-human rights world, a great many areas of activity went largely unregulated. We have discussed how some anti-rights folk are nostalgic for such a 'state of nature'. There, only the fittest or most ruthless survive and thrive. However, we can now assume that at least some of them approve, at least to some degree, of drugs controls, and nuclear power and weapons safety standards.

By the end of May the same year, a number of other similar statements had been released to an anxious world. One in particular, coordinated by the San Francisco-based Center for AI Safety, hit the headlines on account of the many serving captains of the tech industry who were moved to sign it:

> Mitigating the risk of extinction from AI should be a global priority alongside other societal-scale risks such as pandemics and nuclear war.[16]

Open and Fair Justice

The justice system is one of the bedrocks of modern civilization and we have considered how the right to a fair trial – especially but not exclusively – in the face of criminal charges and punishment is, in and of itself, a fundamental civil and political right. It is also essential to the ultimate safeguarding of other freedoms and to the rule of law. The components of this right include the impartiality of the judge or tribunal – and to include a 'jury of one's peers' – in some systems and instances. However, you are also supposed to know the case you have to combat and be able to participate in its hearing, including, where appropriate, with legal representation. There is a presumption that justice be in public. If you are a stranger and unable to speak the local language, there is a vital entitlement to language translation. The trial must be understood if it is to be effective and fair.

Crucially, there is to be 'equality of arms' between the parties to the proceedings. There must also be 'equality before the law' between different people, regardless of financial means and social status, in addition to other factors such as race, sex, faith, age, disability and sexuality that increasingly constitute unlawful discrimination even outside the court room.

Of course, the more opaque day-to-day decisions made about us are, the harder it is to spot their potential illegality, and to challenge them against the relevant legal standards.

Criminal justice is supposed to be the gold standard of procedural fairness on account of the gravest consequences for the accused. These include potential incarceration and even death for still too many people in our modern world. In sharp contrast with, say, the realm of banking or insurance, it has, theoretically at least, long been unacceptable for a court to presume a rich person more worthy or less prone to dishonesty, fraud or theft than their poor neighbour, regardless of what anyone's statistical probabilities might suggest.

Indeed, such is the burden on accusers in a human rights-based criminal trial, that even a defendant's previous convictions are considered irrelevant (or certainly too *prejudicial*) to the present charge, as opposed to any subsequent sentence.

In many parts of the world, Big Tech corporations have now entered and begun to monetize even this most sacred temple of due process. The technology is, for the most part, far less regulated during its design, procurement and deployment than in, for example, the equally corporatized, commercially confidential and potentially dangerous world of pharmaceuticals.

At the beginning of the process, some police forces are even using predictive AI to decide where to deploy precious resources. However, historical structural inequalities on the basis of wealth and race, in particular, mean that the bulk of police data relates to traditionally 'over-policed' communities. The 'garbage in, garbage out' principle will mean that the computer is likely to be fed disproportionate and discriminatory historic stop, arrest, charge and even conviction data. This will lead the police to the poorer parts of town.

They are unlikely to be pointed to the skyscrapers, mansions and luxury hotels where insider dealing, tax fraud and illegal arms deals are more likely to be perpetrated. Sexual and violent crimes happen everywhere but are more easily concealed in more elite neighbourhoods. On the basis that if a trained eye goes looking for crime they will find it, predictive policing very quickly becomes a vicious circle and self-fulfilling prophecy. It feeds the AI more and more of the same.

Cameras and facial recognition technology (FRT) are also becoming the frequent basis for stop and search (or frisk), and even for arrests. On account of the personal profiles of the tech bros who developed and first tested it, this technology is notorious for producing disproportionately unreliable results in relation to people with darker skin tones and women. The 2020 Netflix documentary *Coded Bias* features MIT researcher Joy Buolamwini's now famous accidental discovery in 2016 that commercially available FRT rendered her invisible until she donned a white mask. Once skewed technology is in the hands of institutionally discriminatory uniformed services incapable of offering human correction, it can only turbocharge oppression.

Closed-circuit TV cameras have developed a great deal in recent years. Much of the kit used all over the world, including in the UK, hails from China. It is now capable of providing real-time surveillance in addition to recorded images to its masters, and even – in the case of smart cameras – of sending data back to the manufacturing mother ship.

In law enforcement, such cameras may be used retrospectively, as when images of shoplifting or other crimes are caught on camera and subsequently circulated as part of the investigation. However, they may also form part of real-time police surveillance operations, combined with FRT in public spaces as part of proactive policing. Real-time images of passers-by in the area where the cameras are deployed are matched against a 'watch list' of persons of interest.

In the United Kingdom, there is no specific legislation governing this activity and the police essentially rely upon their own view of the common law and prevailing guidance for their legal authority. I find it very difficult to see how this squares with the requirement that privacy intrusions under Article 8 of the ECHR are 'in accordance with the law'. Regular oversight is limited to the Information Commissioner (charged with enforcing data protection law with its extensive law enforcement exceptions), police-appointed 'ethics committees', and guidance from the National Police Chiefs' Council. These friendly watchdogs do not always bark in the night.[17]

To my knowledge at the time of writing, two UK police forces – London's Metropolitan Police Service and the South Wales Police – have been experimenting with real-time blanket surveillance operations. They procured the technology from the private company of their choice. They compile the criteria for the watch list. They decide what level of technical mitigation should be employed to limit sex and race discrimination in false matches. They decide what level of training their officers should receive. They decide where and when to deploy the technology, and with what 'intelligence-based' justification. This is in dramatic contrast with nearly forty years of legislative authorization for new police powers.[18]

At a closed Metropolitan Police briefing for an invited

audience in April 2023, I was told that London's busy and racially diverse West End shopping district of Oxford Circus had been selected on account of some unpleasant street robberies of Rolex watches. This presentation took place barely two weeks after Baroness Casey's report on the standards and culture of the Metropolitan Police[19] found the force institutionally racist, misogynist and homophobic.

The previous autumn, the Cambridge University Minderoo Centre for Technology and Democracy published an evaluation of three of these operations in London and South Wales during the previous five years.[20] The researchers found all three operations had breached minimal ethical and legal standards for the governance of FRT. Silkie Carlo of the UK civil liberties advocacy group Big Brother Watch describes 'live FRT' as 'suspicionless mass surveillance that turns us all into walking ID cards, subjecting innocent people to biometric police identity checks'.

As a young lawyer in the British Home Office in the 1990s, I witnessed immigration officers 'training' themselves for a more proactive role in immigration enforcement 'in country', not just at the border. I was invited to attend one of their sessions to explain the law, only to find them entertaining each other with role-plays during which white officers mimicked Nigerian accents. During this time, I also came across the case of a young Black Briton with learning disabilities who had been arrested and detained as an illegal entrant. He had managed to produce an identity document, but was nonetheless incarcerated for many months before a female officer new to the case contradicted her colleagues and found the image to be a clear match to the person. I wonder what would have happened if she hadn't just had the more senior male officers to contend with, but the added obstacle of assumed machine neutrality and infallibility as well.

There are now a number of US stories of wrongful police arrests followed by lengthy detention of African Americans on the basis of CCTV images from crime scenes, facial misrecognition and other types of false identification. They include Porcha Woodruff, wrongly arrested and handcuffed in front of her children while eight months pregnant in a dawn raid of her home in Detroit; she was erroneously suspected of robbery and carjacking.[21] US citizens have similarly been excluded from their homeland for long periods because of mistaken identity at the border.

The Windrush scandal[22] in the United Kingdom led to large numbers of Black Britons who came lawfully to the UK from Caribbean former colonies as children being deprived of access to work, benefits, healthcare and even being removed from the country. Their immigration records had been destroyed by the Home Office. Even without the aid of images or AI, they were 'systematically' targeted for unlawful enforcement and dispossession on account of their race. This seems to me a thoroughly British, embryonic version of what legendary Princeton professor Ruha Benjamin calls 'the New Jim Code'.[23]

You might be thinking that a machine would surely be more reliable and less biased than the humans we have relied upon in such matters for so long. However, that assumes so much about the quality of both the code and the data on which the programme is being fed, and about the humans who then apply the calculations that the machines are producing. The literature is full of examples of AI distinguishing pictures of huskies from other dogs on the basis of the circumstantial presence of snow rather than some more exacting feature. No doubt such machine learning could improve with enough time, data and fine-tuning if our discriminatory societies improved first. However, in the context of criminal justice with its presumption of innocence, as with other decisions with enormous consequences for the individual, even a small percentage of false positives is a price we should struggle *not* to pay.

Humans with power over each other may no doubt be biased, corrupt or otherwise unreliable in their judgements. However, they are more likely than either a computer or a distant corporate mogul to reflect heavily upon grave decisions in real time. They are also more likely to face personal consequences for their errors which are easier to scrutinize, detect and challenge.

Humans tasked with checking computerized decisions are likely to become fatigued with boredom and subsequently deskilled. Years of smartphone use have made me far less able to remember telephone numbers. Rather more catastrophic was the 2009 Air France Airbus disaster that cost 228 lives. It is attributed to aircrew too accustomed to autopilot and therefore unable manually to correct machine malfunctions, calmly, and in time. The converse though equally salutary lesson against over-reliance on machines is that of Soviet Air Defence operative Stanislav Petrov. When a nuclear early-warning system erroneously reported a US missile launch in 1983, he exercised personal judgement, broke retaliation protocol and paused until the suspected false alarm was clear. Petrov is sometimes described as 'the man who saved the world'.[24]

AI is already being used in sentencing decisions in many parts of the United States and in prisoner categorization in the UK. Guilt having already been determined at trial, it is argued that determination of future risk based on historic factors is ripe for calculation by an algorithm that never becomes tired, hungry or cynical. Crucially, however, the *computer code* and calculation is developed and owned by corporate contractors rather than the state. In contrast with decades of *legal code* in the form of sentencing statutes, guidance and prison rules, it is shielded from democratic public scrutiny and easy judicial challenge or appeal.

Too Close for Comfort

It's not just algorithmic policing and sentencing tools that present a challenge for both our justice system and rights framework. If Eleanor Roosevelt was correct and human rights begin in 'small places close to home', transparency and redress, alongside empathy and flexibility, are vital at school, work, the bank, the polling station, the hospital and the housing department.

Indeed, they are needed in every place where both civil and political and social and economic rights are first delivered and sometimes violated. In recent years, AI used by US school boards has deprived good teachers of their jobs and excellent students of their deserved grades. It has determined personal credit ratings that have been used beyond bank lending and insurance to determine more general character reliability for the automated sifting of employment applications. This creates the obvious vicious circle in which the poor who have bad credit ratings are then unfairly deprived of the employment opportunities with which to improve them.

The world of financial services in general, and insurance in particular, has traditionally been very private and self-regulated. However, as veteran mathematician Cathy O'Neil describes so compellingly in *Weapons of Math Destruction*,[25] the 2008 financial crash demonstrated the dangers of both AI-led financial markets and insufficient law and regulation to protect poor and middle-income people from a risk-taking industry running out of control.

We have long been used to insurance companies considering factors that would constitute unlawful discrimination in other areas of life. Age and disability are obvious examples, though increasingly worrying in healthcare systems like the USA's, where access to medical provision is so dependent upon having insurance. Just how fair is a contract of insurance between a giant company with access to health profiling data about you and the wider population that you, the subject, lack access to? What if you first learn of the grave risk of a congenital condition, not from your physician, but from the AI that decides you are uninsurable?

Medical diagnosis itself has long benefited from technological advancement. However, false negatives and 'coded bias' against minorities and women have also long been present. Human caution is required to mitigate the risks. I don't mind my smartphone's facial recognition entry system locking me out in bad light or if I yawn. The negative consequence is minimal. I know there is a problem and can simply try again, or use my numerical passcode.

However, in the context of assessing a patient's scan for cancer, the risks of error are grave enough to suggest the belt-and-braces approach of a real human eye *in addition* to the obvious benefits from automation. This is the initial conclusion of exciting Swedish breast cancer research comparing AI-supported screening *followed by* interpretation by one, rather than the usual two, radiologists.[26] In the UK, the National Institute for Health and Care Excellence (NICE), which regulates the use of clinical technology, has since approved some AI to *assist* and speed up, rather than replace, radiotherapists in contouring healthy organs for the purposes of targeting cancer treatment.[27]

Post codes affect both home and driving insurance and, as

in the case of police deployment, without conscious human and human rights interventions, they quickly become proxies for class and race. If such considerations are shielded by commercially confidential software, it becomes much harder for citizens, regulators and legislators to assess the fairness of a policy or practice in order to have any chance of challenging it.

Then, of course, there are the existential questions for our society and democracy posed by the machine replacement of large swathes of human employment on the one hand, and the manipulation of democratic elections by social and other AI-influenced media on the other.

It may seem dystopian, but the threats are already too real. In my lifetime alone, I have witnessed the decimation of industrial workplaces and surrounding communities by globalization. Later, large numbers of lower-level clerical and retail jobs were lost to software. Some suggest that the rapid development of advanced AI will deliver similar blows to even traditionally more prestigious, skilled and remunerative roles in the law, financial sector, creative industries, medicine, and even within science and technology itself.

The delivery of essentially social and economic rights to the means of existence are, for the most part, left to politics and its offshoot, economics. However, if they are neglected for too many people for too long, the cost in human misery and societal breakdown becomes grave. The inevitable social and political unrest is something that the post-war settlement was in no small part seeking to avoid. No doubt, some will take the view that such matters should simply be left to the natural evolution of the market. Others from a range of political persuasions will remember some of the collateral damage of previous periods of industrial transformation.

Debates continue to rage about the role of the state in cushioning the blow to those in employments heading for obsolescence. At the very least, one might hope for some investment towards retraining for the new world of work. Some of us might go further, though, and argue for shorter working hours, minimum incomes, and investment in *social infrastructure* such as education and health and social care for which the state has special responsibility.

Live, as opposed to ever-more synthesized, performance arts and entertainment should be nurtured not cut, by governments seeking to foster greater community. This has been at least part of our economic history, alongside our human rights one. Even corporate consumerism, with its cost-cutting robots, will struggle to sustain its profit model if too large a proportion of the world's population becomes too impoverished to purchase its delights.

Undue influence in democratic elections is perhaps a tougher nut to crack, not least for the lack of transparency and accountability of the technology we are discussing.

The Cambridge Analytica–Facebook scandal of 2018[28] serves as the most high-profile warning of the obvious logic that as modern commercial marketing and political campaigning have so much in common, subversive online methods that were developed to sell products might also be used to influence democratic elections. It is the subversion rather than the selling that is the sin. In the case of Cambridge Analytica, the shady consultancy illegally acquired the personal data of up to 87 million Facebook users by way of a personality profiling quiz accessed by a smaller number of their friends. The boasts of some and allegations of others suggest the company then used personality-specific targeted ads, some disguised as newsfeed, based on falsehoods and preying on the vulnerable, to influence the 2016 US presidential vote.

Whatever the whole truth, the answer is perhaps to begin with more general human rights principles for the internet, AI and robotics. Then we must drill down into more area-specific challenges, whether in various types of commerce, essential services, justice, and even elections themselves.

Take Back Control

The genie will not re-enter the bottle, nor, in my view, need that be our aspiration. Just as a carving knife may feed or kill a family and a jar of pills be pain relief or suicide, we must learn better to apply and regulate our new technologies. Human rights principles can help with this pressing global task.

The internet can no longer be such an ungoverned or illegitimately governed space. The East India Company once brought great riches to the British Empire, but lacked democratic accountability to the people of Britain, let alone the subcontinent whose name it bore. The same can be said of the titans of Silicon Valley. They are essentially unaccountable to the vast majority of Americans, let alone to the workers and consumers of the nations in which they mine, harvest and profit. Indeed, the better analogy is that these corporations are more like empires than mere companies of previous centuries. Logos replace flags and billionaires are kings. Shareholders are perhaps some pale imitation of a new electorate. Suffrage is once more far from universal.

Surely it is time for all transnational corporations, whether in tech or other fields, to be more directly subject to international human rights treaties that have previously been left to nation states to transpose into domestic law and enforce? This would require a new global treaty to supplement the various continental instruments discussed in Chapter 2. The precise framing of remedies would have to be sensitive to any limitations faced by such enterprises in various jurisdictions. However, with the values themselves, even their impressive PR machines might struggle to argue.

The suggestion obviously begs the question as to whether existing human rights as articulated in the various covenants and conventions are currently sufficient to meet the challenges outlined and anticipated. In such difficult times for human rights in general, I am generally a subscriber to the 'stick don't twist' theory of not exposing precious norms to possible dilution. However, there might be something to be said for the idea that, just as war and climate catastrophe justify specific treaty provision, no less is required in this enormous area of our contemporary human experience.

We've touched on the limitations of the online-as-offline paradigm.[29] Our human rights, as internationally settled and articulated nearly three quarters of a century ago, have a great deal still to offer. However, just as the world community subsequently moved to deal more specifically with the various forms of discrimination, with child protection and the prohibition of torture, it could mobilize again for the challenges and opportunities of cyberspace.

Existing rights against degrading treatment and discrimination and for privacy and due process could be extrapolated more precisely with the online and AI contexts in mind. New or newly expressed rights to access the internet, or indeed to a final *human decision* in a number of key spheres of our lives, could be specifically enshrined.[30]

As for AI in particular, the European Commission's Ethics

Guidelines for Trustworthy AI[31] seem a very good starting point. They set out seven ethical requirements to ensure:

1. Human agency and oversight.
2. Technical robustness and safety.
3. Privacy and data governance.
4. Transparency – including the need to ensure that humans understand who or what they are interacting with.
5. Diversity, non-discrimination and fairness – including accessibility to all.
6. Societal and environmental well-being for the benefits of humanity, including future generations.
7. Accountability, including 'mechanisms . . . to ensure responsibility and accountability for AI systems and their outcomes'. In this paradigm, the Commission includes 'auditability', enabling the 'assessment of algorithms, data and design processes' especially in 'safety-critical applications'. Adequate redress is also supposed to be a key component in this principle.

Rather than merely remaining a voluntary set of standards, these will form the basis for a new legally binding AI Act. However, this approach should not be restricted to the EU. Like-minded democratic states must surely see the value of building trust in their technology, better to reap its potential social and economic rewards. In advance of such hard-won transnational, let alone global, consensus, there is a great deal that individual nation states, ethical citizens and businesses might do to move things along.

Even a single legal jurisdiction, visionary business or NGO could begin 'kite-marking' or vetting and approving AI tools for various purposes. With time, investment and expertise, this 'brand' might become internationally trusted, rather like Swiss watches, British courts or *The New York Times*.

Of course, the public procurement of AI involving taxpayers' money and people's rights should be much more tightly held by responsible governments. They would be wise to develop their own software, take proprietorial control of the algorithms and keep safe custody of any personal data. It is frankly laughable that local police chiefs should be able to go shopping for this kit, or even have it 'given' to them by commercial developers hungry for data with which to experiment.

If pharmaceuticals can be tightly regulated and approved by state agencies, so can AI. We might further learn from our follies in Big Pharma, where public and philanthropic dollars fund the research and billionaires take the intellectual property and the profits. Given the sensitivities of the products and their use, there is a strong argument for the existence of at least some publicly owned companies in this space, and even for the publication and approval of relevant computer code in schedules to legislation.

In an ideal world, I would advocate:

- New binding international conventions governing the internet, responsible AI and the direct human rights responsibilities of all corporations.
- International and domestic agencies and laws for the enforcement of these treaties and for the regulation of cyberspace; including the prior vetting, approval and banning of certain new technologies and their particular applications.
- More multidisciplinary academic communities of the kind that are already emerging in world-class universities. Almost a reflection of ancient scholarship,

> these combine the disciplines of philosophy, law, science and technology. However, they must be as independent as possible of huge vested interests, if they are better to supply and inform the industry, legislators and regulators of tomorrow.

It is far too soon, for me at least, to imagine artificial intelligence of a nature that justifies a panoply of 'robot rights'. I appreciate that time may yet come. However, the companies that own the machines are also artificial creatures. They enjoy legal personality and certain rights and duties on behalf of their human masters. They have outgrown the jurisdictions that first incorporated them, so new and further duties are clearly required. For the foreseeable future, we must seek better to understand, harness and regulate technological tools, so as not to become oppressed by them. This is the very cutting edge of human ingenuity and human rights.

6.
War and Peace

Never think that war, no matter how necessary nor how justified, is not a crime.

Ernest Hemingway[1]

Such are the tensions between our wars, laws, rights and humanity that it would take many libraries even to begin to do them justice. Ideally, those shelves and volumes would be filled for the most part with the first-hand testimony of generations of the living and the dead. Volunteer and conscript soldiers, sailors and airmen, civilian casualties and their orphans would all share their experience in those pages. Walls of paintings and photographs could only attempt to reveal the permanent scars to people, families and societies. Inevitably, leaders, lawyers, journalists and activists of all stripes are rather more prolific in their written output. Still, we cannot properly consider the contested benefits of human rights in our contemporary world without dipping our toes into the dangerous waters of the contribution of fundamental freedoms to rethinking violent conflict and its aftermath.

We must remember that human rights are in no small part supposed to be part of a language of negotiation that should make it less necessary for the vulnerable and abused to have to resort to violence against their oppressors, whether across geographical borders or within them. However, to be valuable and viable, rights must restrict rulers as much as the ruled.

Rights sceptics predictably paint a grotesque picture of brave service men and women sent into combat with 'one hand tied behind their back'. The suggested injustice is of often young and junior personnel living in fear of 'lawfare' waged via endless complaints and investigations, with the possibility of grave legal sanction years after the fact. However, these very critics are almost equally dismissive of the occasions when the same uniformed people are abused by comrades and superiors, or sent to war with grossly inadequate training or equipment, and make human rights arguments in relation to their own ill-treatment.

Claims by foreign nationals 'over there' are dismissed as coming from vanquished insurgents and their ambulance-chasing lawyers. Challenges from returned veterans 'over here' are said to be the disloyal whinging of the young or the 'soft'. They are accused of too readily equating military service with civilian employment and its caricatured rights to air conditioning, bespoke coffee and the like.

However, the criticisms and the tropes must nonetheless be addressed. They are so easily deployed as an argument, not just for limiting the role of rights in conflict, but for diluting or dismantling fundamental universal human rights everywhere and altogether.

The 'one hand tied' metaphor is a powerful one, not least for being coined and shared by some of our greatest jurists[2] in explicit acknowledgement of the way in which any rules-based order will inevitably sometimes disadvantage the law-abiding in the short term.

Violence is of course ever-present in nature. Nonetheless,

millennia of human civilization have attempted to constrain its use. Children brought up in the most loving and law-abiding families will sometimes resort to physical confrontations with one another, especially when very young or otherwise disempowered. Still, we try to teach them to do otherwise.

Few of us could not imagine defending ourselves or our loved ones from an assailant. Indeed, the criminal law would be the proverbial ass if it did not recognize self-defence and the defence of others as justification for violence. However, such personal defences tend to be tightly drawn as to both the nature of the threat and the proportionality of the human response.

I might wield my kitchen knife to see off a burglar. Yet if they take the hint and flee, I will struggle in most criminal courts of the world if I chase the escaping intruder way beyond my threshold, down the road, and inflict my own rough justice upon them. Nor should the law look kindly on my breaking down my neighbour's door with suspicion that the criminal was hiding within, or even if I reasonably believed that the place was a base for the planning of many a local burglary.

A pacifist view of what is often called the 'domestic analogy'[3] is that it simply does not hold for 'widespread violence with a political motive'.[4] In my example I have rights, agency and imminent fear. By contrast, wars, whether within countries and continents or across them, inevitably create considerable distance between the controlling minds in authority[5] and the people required to put themselves and others on the line. The brunt is borne by those who must follow orders and be in harm's way, and those who are the civilian collateral damage. Further, these wars have always been fought or furthered on much broader grounds than mere self-defence.

Renowned war poet and Military Cross recipient Siegfried Sassoon wrote in 1917:

> I believe that the war upon which I entered as a war of defence and liberation has now become a war of aggression and conquest. I believe that the purposes for which I and my fellow soldiers entered upon this war should have been so clearly stated as to have made it impossible to change them and that had this been done the objects which actuated us would now be attainable by negotiation.[6]

Conversely, believers in just wars, most famously Hugo Grotius, might argue that the obvious reason why I should not take the law into my own hands in the burglar example is due to the presence of legitimate and functioning policing and criminal justice systems in rule of law-based states. In the absence of world cops and courts, however, nations have long had – and, some would argue, still have – no choice but to wage war as a means of furthering their 'interests' and alliances for mutual security. Even before the outbreak of World War II, there were many critics of the First Great War who by then took the opposite view in light of Axis aggression.

However, these national interests have always included the enrichment and other advancement of 'one's own' people over those of other nations. Here we find echoes of some of the universalist versus nationalist arguments for and against human rights that we considered earlier. Via war, nationalists again invite perverse and even catastrophic consequences for all people, including those they claim as their own.[7]

Still, just as human rights are the monopoly of neither the left nor the right, they are far from being the preserve of anyone on an equally long and complex pacifist-to-militarist spectrum.

Human Rights and the Law of War

The Law of War governs its justifications and conduct. It is of far older provenance than our modern conception of human rights. One irony is that rights sceptics – so often nationalist in outlook – will bolster their argument with a robust defence of an exclusive role for the law of war, otherwise known as international humanitarian law (IHL). They do this even though rights necessarily have their origins far closer to home. It is lazy, if convenient, to see IHL and human rights as the law of war and peace respectively. This attempt at clear division is problematic for a number of reasons, not least the fast and ever-changing nature of contemporary violent conflict, and the way in which it seems increasingly to lack the visible declarations, uniforms, insignia and endings of yesteryear.

Sometimes, military hawks resist even the application of IHL, such as in the historic conflicts in Northern Ireland and Gaza, for fear of inadvertently legitimating insurgencies and rebellions by treating them like the traditional armies of recognized opposing states.

In the War on Terror, all law and language was deliberately blurred to the point of destruction in order to dehumanize enemies and even some foreign civilians. 'Unlawful combatants' were neither prisoners of war nor criminal defendants awaiting charge and trial. 'Enhanced interrogation' became a euphemism for torture. In a clear breach of international law, torture was 'redefined' by government lawyers and executive instructions to exclude treatment that did not quite lead to 'serious physical injury, such as organ failure, impairment of bodily function, or even death'.[8]

While rights critics complain of 'lawfare' as a malicious

and mischievous weaponization of law, we might counter that language itself may be refashioned as a weapon of the powerful against the vulnerable. In the words of George Orwell, it can be:

> designed to make lies sound truthful and murder respectable, and to give the appearance of solidity to pure wind.[9]

The human rights and IHL strands in law and legal thinking are inevitably in constant conversation, and occasional argument, with each other. However, since at least World War II, they follow the same ultimately humanitarian instincts. The dialogue between them becomes increasingly complementary, and has even led to some merging over time. The vital human right not to be arbitrarily deprived of your life under Article 6 of the International Covenant on Civil and Political Rights will be read as being subject to the law of war in a war zone.

Both systems prohibit torture, but crucially, and in contrast with the sophistry of former White House lawyers in the early 2000s, its definition comes from the 1984 *human rights* instrument, the UN Convention against Torture:

> For the purposes of this Convention, the term 'torture' means any act by which severe pain or suffering, whether physical or mental, is intentionally inflicted on a person for such purposes as obtaining from him or a third person information or confession, punishing him for an act he or a third person is suspected of having committed, or intimidating or coercing him or a third person, or for any reason based on discrimination of any kind, when such pain or suffering is inflicted by or at the instigation of or with the consent or acquiescence of a public official or other person acting in an official capacity.

Lawyers sometimes refer to this mixing and matching of applicable law as identifying the *lex specialis* or rules of most specific relevance. Few explain this particular legal cocktail better than Professor Thomas W. Smith in his *Human Rights and War Through Civilian Eyes*.[10]

> Human rights and humanitarian law are not two stone tablets, one we consult in war, the other in peace. The regimes often borrow and trade ideas. Nor are human rights as absolute or otherworldly as critics claim. The movement is hardly pacifist. For every human rights activist calling for an end to war there are two clamouring for armed intervention to protect rights.

He goes on to discuss the comparisons, contrasts and common ground between the two traditions. I think we can distil and debate a number of observations from his work.

Firstly, while human rights emerged from the struggle been oppressed and disadvantaged *people and their rulers*, the law of war sprang from the customary practices of belligerent powers and, later, the treaties concluded multilaterally *between sovereign states*. Rights are fought for from the *bottom up* (as in revolutions, elections and campaigns), whereas IHL is ultimately more *horizontal and reciprocal* in nature. I would go further and suggest that in a pre-democratic era, when rulers waged so much war for the expansion of their dominions or the distraction of those in their domain, it made obvious sense to strike 'gentlemen's agreements' (around, for example, the treatment and exchange of prisoners), aimed at making those campaigns a little more convenient and attractive to those who would ultimately pay the price.

Secondly, rights (such as to fair trials) were domestic norms that were codified in international law. IHL (governing belligerent conduct between nation states) was international from the start.

Thirdly, from a philosophical perspective, human rights belong to people and are universal in nature. In assuming the inevitability of war, IHL leans towards a statist ethic and a national security framework.

Fourthly, rights are animated by the voices of victims declaring clear violations of rights that accordingly demand vindication and remedy. By contrast, the law of war is ameliorative rather than absolute. It calls for a place for charity and mercy, for example towards civilians, amid what is seen as the brutal necessity of war.

Fifthly, IHL traditionally governed the just causes of war (like self-defence), as well as its just conduct. By contrast, human rights advocates have been historically slower to enter arguments about the instigation of war itself. Instead, human rights provide a list of specific ends (like elections and food) to which people are entitled. These might form a blueprint for a new or reconstituted society in the aftermath of war.

Finally, while both regimes observe *proportionality*, they 'weigh the economy of violence' on a different scale. Under the law of war, the anticipated harm to civilian life or property must be consonant with the military advantages. Crucially, these are chosen by the belligerent powers themselves. In the world of human rights, violence is allowed only to prevent greater rights interference. Rights offer a tighter discipline in the face of military demands.

However, we must acknowledge that in recent decades, human rights advocates have become sharply divided over the question of 'humanitarian intervention'. This is a thorny question to which we will have to return.

The Law of War

International humanitarian law has overlapping sources in the form of treaties and conventions, custom and practice, and general principles. Customary international law binds states automatically, with no signing up required.

The essential principles are military necessity, distinction, proportionality, humanity and honour (sometimes referred to by way of the increasingly archaic term 'chivalry').

Military necessity requires that an attack should be intended to help in the defeat of the enemy. It must be aimed at a legitimate military objective. However, such objectives are ultimately chosen by the belligerent power itself.

Distinction requires that the belligerent distinguish between combatants and civilians.

Proportionality requires that harm to civilians or civilian property should not be excessive in relation to the direct military advantage being sought. The belligerent chooses the military objective, so proportionality becomes a more flexible test than required in the context of necessary interferences with qualified rights. It is looser still when compared with the strict necessity test for derogating from human rights in time of war or other public emergencies.

Humanity is about not using arms designed to cause maximum human suffering or using any arms in a manner designed to do so.

Honour is intended to suggest a form of mutual respect between adversaries, almost in recognition of the way that those on each side are ultimately dutifully following the orders of their own state authorities. In particular, it prohibits taking advantage of an enemy's adherence to the law.

So, it would, for example, prohibit pretending to be injured or dead or to surrender, only subsequently to ambush the other side.

The 1945 UN Charter now governs when war is lawful. It confines this to two circumstances only: when a member state or group of member states acts in self-defence, or when the Security Council[11] authorizes military action for the purposes of maintaining security.

The Security Council is the UN organ charged with this function and it comprises ten temporary members elected for two-year terms and five permanent members. Each member has a vote and a majority of nine to six is required. However, each permanent member is also in possession of a veto. The permanent members of the Security Council are China, France, the Russian Federation (the USSR until 1990), the United Kingdom and the United States.

One need not have the keenest eye for twentieth-century history to spot the notional 'winners' of World War II as those given primary responsibility for securing the new world order after that terrible global conflict. Nor need one be an expert in contemporary international relations to perceive a potential design flaw in allowing a security veto to a fixed list of powers who are just as capable of posing threats to peace as of bringing peaceful resolution to conflict.

The Charter was followed in 1946 by the Judgement of the International Military Tribunal at Nuremberg and in 1947 by the Nuremberg Principles. Nineteen forty-eight saw the establishment of the United Nations Convention on the Prevention and Punishment of the Crime of Genocide.

Nineteen forty-nine brought the four Geneva Conventions. The first is for the Amelioration of the Condition of the Wounded and Sick in Armed Forces in the Field. The second is for the Amelioration of the Wounded, Sick and Shipwrecked Members of Armed Forces at Sea. The third is Relative to the Treatment of Prisoners of War, and the fourth, for the Protection of Civilian Persons in Time of War.

The 1971 Zagreb Resolution governs the Conditions of Application of Humanitarian Rules of Armed Conflict to Hostilities in which United Nations Forces May be Engaged. This was followed by the 1974 Declaration on the Protection of Women and Children in Emergency and Armed Conflict.

Accountability

An obvious practical distinction between human rights law and IHL lies in the means of holding those who violate them to account. IHL has sometimes been investigated and enforced by ad hoc international tribunals, most famously those established in Germany and Japan after World War II.

This precedent was later followed by the establishment of tribunals at The Hague in the Netherlands and Arusha, Tanzania, to deal with allegations arising from conflicts in the Balkans and Rwanda in the 1990s. In the former case, Yugoslav President Slobodan Milošević became the first ever head of state to face such a trial. While he died in his prison cell, having defended himself personally and consistently denouncing the legality of the trial on the grounds that it had not been agreed by the UN, the subsequent findings of ethnic cleansing and failure to prevent genocide make real the possibility of instigators of wars, rather than junior foot soldiers, being held accountable for gross violations of IHL.

There have also been so-called mixed courts and tribunals with jurisdiction to deal with both alleged international and domestic crimes in Kosovo, Bosnia and Herzegovina, East Timor, Sierra Leone, Cambodia and Lebanon.

War crimes, including torture, genocide and crimes against humanity, are regarded as so grave that all states are also required to assert criminal jurisdiction over them, regardless of where in the world they occurred and who they were perpetrated by or against.

In 2005, at London's Central Criminal Court, the Old Bailey, Afghan warlord Faryadi Sarwar Zardad was found guilty of a number of heinous crimes against civilians ten years earlier in Afghanistan. He had fled to the UK from the Taliban, but came to notice after BBC reports and an international campaign. It was the first case of its kind under the Convention against Torture, requiring video links to the British Embassy in Kabul, and the protection of victim and witness identities for fear of retaliation. It took two trials for a jury to reach a verdict.

In 2002, the International Criminal Court was established in The Hague to take up cases that states may be unable or unwilling to investigate and prosecute themselves. However, dozens of countries have failed fully to accept its jurisdiction, putting their citizens beyond easy reach. These include permanent Security Council Members China and the United States. Their argument for this position is our old friend – national sovereignty.

Practical Relief

In any event, we can see that in contrast with the direct access to justice requirement for victims of human rights abuses, the initiative for acting on the violations of IHL lies very much with states and those organs of the international community more likely to be swayed by pragmatic political considerations.

It is therefore understandable that those who have suffered may sometimes prefer to find their own lawyers and bring their own claims in either domestic or international human rights courts. This may feel preferable to lobbying nation states and the international community, perhaps for decades, in the hope of seeing some form of redress.

IHL courts and tribunals may provide greater moral satisfaction in specifically finding guilt of war crimes against individuals. Nonetheless, the finding of human rights violations, not least if combined with some material compensation, may be significant help to victims or their bereaved families. This is no less logical than when victims of crime who feel let down by the inaction of local police and prosecutors bring claims against the authorities or even the alleged criminals in ordinary courts.

Another attraction of seeking redress in human rights courts is the possibility of urgent interim orders being issued, even as a war is still being waged. On 24 February 2022, the Russian Federation invaded and occupied parts of Ukraine in a major escalation of the Russo-Ukrainian War, which had been ongoing since 2014 when Russia annexed Crimea from Ukraine and began supporting pro-Russian separatists in the Donbas region. There are allegations of rape and murder of civilians, and looting of their property, as well as the torture of Ukrainian military prisoners by Russian and pro-Russian forces in the conflict.

European Court of Human Rights Rule 39 allows a judge of the Court to 'indicate to the parties any interim measure which they consider should be adopted in the interests of the parties or of the proper conduct of the proceedings'. It is the Court's practice that such measures should only be granted where there is an 'imminent risk of irreparable harm'.

Most orders of this kind are made in expulsion cases for fear that potential deportation or extradition from a Council of Europe state might lead to someone being tortured or killed elsewhere. In its Illegal Migration Act 2023, the UK Government legislated domestically so as to permit UK Ministers to ignore Rule 39 measures in relation to the removal of asylum seekers arriving in small boats. The crossing of this Rubicon by a permanent member of the Security Council and leading architect of the Council of Europe is unfortunate to say the least when Rule 39 Orders have been issued to prevent Russia imposing the death penalty on surrendered members of Ukraine's armed forces.[12]

Russia was expelled from the Council of Europe in 2022, leaving a question mark over the jurisdiction of the Convention and the European Court of Human Rights. However, it must be hoped that the combination of these clear interim orders and the possibility of war crimes trials at the conclusion of the conflict will dissuade Russian forces from executing prisoners of war contrary to both the Geneva Conventions and the ECHR. This is an obvious example of the considerable benefits that human rights and IHL each bring to the other.

The Empire Strikes Back

Of course, this developing reach of law into the theatre of war is extremely irritating to some states. Their lawyers will inevitably attempt to knock out claims on procedural grounds relating to a lack of connection between people or places, so as not to have to defend their substantive actions in courts that become world stages.

Some domestic and international human rights instruments

have jurisdictional clauses appearing to limit their responsibility to particular territory. Others are silent. However, given the history of grave humanitarian and human rights abuses in various 'no man's lands' – from the high seas of previous centuries to the black sites of the twenty-first – we can see the obvious dangers in an overly narrow approach to jurisdiction. Hence the UN Human Rights Committee, charged with monitoring compliance with the International Covenant on Civil and Political Rights, issued this pronouncement in 2004:

> The enjoyment of Covenant rights is not limited to citizens of State Parties but must also be available to all individuals regardless of nationality or statelessness, such as asylum seekers, refugees, migrant workers and other persons, who may find themselves in the territory or subject to the jurisdiction of the State Party. This principle also applies to those *within the power or effective control of the forces of a State Party acting outside its territory, regardless of the circumstances in which such power or effective control was obtained.*[13]

Similarly, in the *Banković* case of 2001,[14] while ruling against jurisdiction in relation to a number of lethal NATO air strikes on Belgrade, the European Court of Human Rights nonetheless pointed towards 'control' as the basis for its legal jurisdiction to consider violations.

This is important in moving, however tentatively, from the assertion of legal jurisdiction over land to practical control over people as a basis for state and court responsibility for violations. It also makes crystal clear that the illegality of a war or occupation will not have the perverse effect of creating effective impunity for the abuses that follow. This approach has arguably increased incrementally over the subsequent two decades. The Inter-American Commission on Human Rights (IACHR), an organ of the Organization of American States, has taken the more expansive analysis of 'control over reasonably foreseeable consequences', including of a missile strike, rather than only for land or people.[15]

Dalia Palombo is a leading expert on the relationship between *extraterritoriality* where states are legally responsible for acts beyond their borders, *transnationality* or legal disputes arising across international borders, and *universality*, which is supposed to be a key philosophical feature of human rights. She suggests that even the control paradigm is too timid and tortuous to deliver effectively against so many contemporary global human rights challenges.[16] With an analysis that cuts across public international law (in which both humanitarian and human rights laws sit) and private international law (or 'conflict of laws' and the rules governing cross-border disputes between private parties), she points to an increasing number of cases where private law is delivering human rights outcomes.

Such developments provoke a great deal of political and rhetorical pushback from military hawks and rights sceptics. Still, it is important to remember that the European Court of Human Rights grants a wide margin of appreciation to states that derogate from certain rights in 'war or other public emergency'. Further, in echoes of the way that the law began to bite upon the transatlantic slave trade, the most anxious scrutiny has been reserved for the moments when, in the words of Nicholas Mercer, 'a man is reduced to captivity'.[17]

A New Hope

Reverend Nicholas Mercer is a Church of England priest. As Lieutenant Colonel Mercer, he was the first Command Legal Adviser in the British Army to have to consider the European Convention on the ground in an international armed conflict – the 2003 Iraq War. Contrary to the views and direction of the Government not to consider Convention rights, Mercer took the opposite view of the implications of *Banković*. He was subsequently vindicated by the courts and says:

> The Convention has had a very positive effect, not least because it has greatly assisted prisoners of war who were subjected to illegal interrogation techniques and mistreatment in Iraq. It has held the Government to account for this and ensured an independent inquiry was held into all the deaths of Iraqi nationals held in UK custody. All of this has greatly improved the condition of prisoners ever since. It has also held the UK to account for prisoners captured by UK forces even when handed over to a third party. It has ensured the proportionate use of force by the UK when acting as the *de facto* public authority after the cessation of hostilities. As a result of the Government being properly held to account, since the end of the Iraq War, there have been endless attempts by the UK Government to shake off their Convention obligations. All of these have come to naught to date.
>
> It is often put about by the Government that the Convention affects Commanders on the battlefield. It does no such thing. The Commanders' discretion on the battlefield is in no way impacted other than in the way they treat their prisoners. In that regard it is undoubtedly a force for good. The ECHR also

> acts as a safety net when there are attempts to limit the scope of the Geneva Conventions. Above all, it holds the Government to account for any illegal activity, such as rendition or complicity in torture or inhuman treatment, that it believes it can get away with. These are not theoretical scenarios. They have already occurred.[18]

An infamous case to which Mercer refers is that of Baha Mousa, a twenty-six-year-old Iraqi civilian, a hotel receptionist, who was arrested by soldiers of the First Battalion of the Queen's Lancashire Regiment, detained, tortured and beaten to death, after a police-style raid on his place of work.[19] It is very far from the traditional battlefield paradigm and highlights the dangers of requiring ill-trained and battle-scarred soldiers to police civilians amid or even in the aftermath of more conventional war.

In the words of the judge during the 2007 court martial of the seven soldiers charged over Mousa's death, those involved 'closed ranks'. The surviving detainees were understandably confused and unable to give firm identification since they were hooded for much of their ordeal. The only conviction was that of Corporal Donald Payne, who entered a guilty plea to abusing prisoners, and was sentenced to one year in prison and discharged from the Army. So international humanitarian Geneva Conventions, national Queen's Regulations and a domestic court martial (with its necessarily high standard of proof) were never going to achieve a vindication of these gravest of human rights abuses. Thomas W. Smith's comment on the case is that 'military justice is to justice what military music is to music'.[20]

Nonetheless, one can see an obvious public policy argument for holding states and their leaders, not foot soldiers, to account when violations are systemic, rather than frolics of the 'few bad apples' so often blamed by those in charge.

This abuse was then the subject of years of human rights litigation and inquiry. The European Court of Human Rights expanded on the UK courts' more limited version of the control principle – covering just Mousa, who was killed in prison. The Court included other civilians who had been shot by UK security patrols on the streets or in raids of their homes. There was a procedural obligation to investigate the civilian deaths that had been breached by the UK authorities.[21]

Indeed, a judge in the case remarked on how distasteful it would be for a state's forces to be liable for the unlawful killing of a civilian prisoner, but immune if they chose to shoot them before arrest.[22] It further revealed the scale of the problem with military training and instruction and the way that five torture techniques – forced standing in stress positions, hooding, noise, sleep and food deprivation – that had been banned in the context of the Northern Ireland Troubles were revived.[23]

Just as governments will deliberately choose to blur the line between the enforcement of law and prosecution of war in dealing with terrorism, there can be very real and practical problems when military forces are left to enforce or re-establish the rule of law once it has been obliterated. This is a reason for keeping hold of human rights values in conflict, but also perhaps for being rather slower to go to war, and more mindful of the responsibilities of its aftermath.

Friendly Fire

Another reason why the military should not be a rights-free zone is the protection offered to those in armed service themselves.

Despite the clear violation of both customary international law and any number of specific humanitarian and human rights obligations, many states still enlist child soldiers for direct conflict or for use as spies, cooks and sex slaves. The martial law closing of ranks that we saw working against civilian victims in the Mousa case can also work against the victims of physical and sexual assault within the service itself. Conversely, the supervision of ordinary and higher rights courts has been crucial to improving the fairness of procedure for those accused in courts-martial systems. This has benefited the independence and impartiality of those tribunals in particular.[24]

The lawyer–soldier divide that makes for such effective political bluster is far from accurate on the ground. Many a service person, veteran or military family has needed resort to law and lawyers in their defence, or when seeking redress or compensation in relation to their abuse or neglect. Though a shining example of a military lawyer, Nicholas Mercer is far from alone. Uniformed lawyers on both sides of the Atlantic fought to uphold human rights and the rule of law in the War on Terror, including by representing both official prisoners and dehumanized detainees.

Aaron Sorkin's 1989 play *A Few Good Men*[25] and its now legendary 1992 screen version[26] seem almost quaint given the military brutality of barely a decade later. For highlighting the crucial values of so many military lawyers in opposing exceptionalism, it was prophetic nonetheless.

Cat and Mouse

Still, there is no end to the energy and ingenuity of governments when attempting the great escape from the law. Whether successful or not, the loud and rhetorical public arguments may be seen by some to be vote-winners in themselves. In 2021, the UK Government secured the passage of its Overseas Operations (Service Personnel and Veterans) Act.[27] It creates a statutory presumption against prosecution of current or past armed service personnel for offences in the course of their duty after five years.

When first passed by the House of Commons, this presumption against prosecution included war crimes, crimes against humanity, genocide and torture. However, these gravest of human rights and humanitarian abuses were excluded from the legislation in the House of Lords. A flamboyant provision to require the Government to consider derogating from human rights was also jettisoned in the second chamber.

No genuine victim nor innocent defendant would wish that a criminal trial take place more than five years after the relevant events. Nonetheless, many very serious crimes come to light or to trial beyond this time period. Further, given the various difficulties in uncovering military abuses and the fact that these investigations and prosecutions are in the hands of the state authorities themselves, it seems particularly self-serving to legislate in this way.

The House of Commons debates were less than edifying and an extreme example of the politics of waving khaki and flags so as to denigrate lawyers and the law. In addition to the five-year presumptive time limit on prosecutions, the Act creates an absolute six-year limitation period for bringing civil claims in relation to injury or death relating to armed service overseas. Ironically for legislation championed as *defending soldiers against lawyers*, this provision extends the time bar to claims by military personnel and veterans against the Government.

Weapons Questions

Any consideration of rights and violent conflict must include the role and responsibility of manufacturing and trade, in abuses that are perpetrated by governments and non-state actors all over the world. On an interconnected planet, should those who make and profit from the means of death and cruelty really be able to escape responsibility for their use by others? Should it matter whether the organization benefiting is a state or private body?

The UK courts have already answered my first question in the negative. The Court of Appeal found that the Government acted unlawfully in selling arms to Saudi Arabia without properly investigating whether these might be used against civilians in Yemen in breach of international humanitarian law.[28] In *Nevsun Resources Ltd v Araya*,[29] the Canadian Supreme Court arguably went even further in relation to both of my questions. In a case about Eritrean military conscripts being allegedly subject to slavery and torture in a mining operation by the subsidiary of a Canadian company, the Court allowed both transnationality and potential corporate liability for gross breaches of international human rights law. In her now famous opinion, Justice Abella began:

> This appeal involves the application of modern international human rights law, the phoenix that rose from the ashes of World War II and declared global war on human rights abuses. Its mandate was to prevent breaches of internationally accepted norms. Those norms were not meant to be theoretical aspirations or legal luxuries, but moral

imperatives and legal necessities. Conduct that undermined the norms was to be identified and addressed.

Two years later, Mexico sued Smith & Wesson and other gun manufacturers in a US court for facilitating arms traffic across the border when this would result in human rights abuses there.[30] Dalia Palombo predicts and indeed recommends more of the same judicial confidence, on the braver and more logically coherent basis of universality. Indeed, it would seem counterintuitive to allow and require universal *criminal* jurisdiction for the gravest abuses, without permitting the *civil* claims more likely to compensate victims, hold controlling minds to account, and change the behaviour of corporations in particular, by focusing them on the bottom line.

The noble tradition of banning certain inhuman weapons in war dates back to Abraham Lincoln's Civil War Lieber Code in 1863. This became a foundation for The Hague Conventions of 1899 and 1907, much of which are now customary international law. Further international arms agreements are to be found in the Geneva Conventions of 1925 and 1949, the 1972 Biological Weapons Convention, 1979 Convention on Certain Conventional Weapons, 1993 Chemical Weapons Convention, 1997 Ottawa Treaty, 2008 Convention on Cluster Munitions, and a number of others.

It may seem strange to ban certain classes of weapons from the inherently deadly activity of war. However, this mirrors human rights thinking in making a distinction between the essential but ultimately qualified right to life, and the absolute rule against torture and inhuman and degrading treatment. Weapons that have been banned as a class are those seen to cause unnecessary cruelty and suffering, especially to civilians.

These include poisonous gases, fragments that cannot be detected by x-ray, land mines, incendiary and blinding weapons, expanding and poisoned bullets, cluster bombs and biological weapons.

In recent years, unmanned aerial vehicles (UAVs), have become increasingly ubiquitous in surveillance and weapons transmission as well as various peacetime uses. Termed 'drones' after their insect-like humming sound, they have been controversial and, without international consensus, cause some complex challenges to traditional international humanitarian legal principles.

The ease with which they may be deployed at long range, with little or no risk to the operator, may challenge more archaic notions of chivalry. The fact that their operation may feel more like video gaming than warfare to a young operator on the other side of the world may lead to a quicker dehumanization of the enemy. In many cases, they are operated by non-military personnel.

Arguments rage about the precision of drone attacks and whether they really put fewer or more civilians at risk for the purposes of differentiation and proportionality. They have certainly led to a greater, or greater open, use of the targeted killing of enemies, and the possible blurring of the line between the potentially lawful targeting of senior combatants in war zones, when for example arrest is impossible, and extraterritorial, extrajudicial and unlawful assassinations outside them.

From a purely human rights point of view, the issue is potentially more straightforward. If the drone attack is not a lawful act of war, it must satisfy another specific legal basis for the use of lethal force. The right to life requires meeting the test of strict necessity for killing instead of arresting, for the protection of others in, for example, an anti-terror or other law-enforcement or peace-keeping operation.

New Camouflage

The use of civilian intelligence services, private contractors and covert special forces in either traditional military or policing operations is a development that human rights are well capable of responding to. States will undoubtedly be held responsible for all these formulations, and rightly so. Just as militia cannot become civilians by giving up their uniforms while cleaving to their guns, Vladimir Putin and the Russian state will in due course be held accountable for the activities of the mercenaries of the Wagner Group, at least before this close contractor went rogue and turned on its client regime.[31] However, we have also seen how other private bodies all over the world may increasingly feel the long arm of human rights law, and, to my mind, rightly so.

Rights thinking will also have to adapt to the deliberate use and undermining of technological infrastructure as a tactic of civil or international war. In requiring consensus by way of agreed custom or specifically negotiated conventions, IHL alone may be less nimble in response to threats from hacks to a rival community's communications, banking, electoral or electrical systems. In being focused on outcomes for both civil and political and social and economic and cultural rights, rather than the precise method of any violation, the human rights framework may continue to serve in both guiding the peaceful and law-abiding in their defensive approaches, and holding lawless belligerents to account.

Humanitarian Intervention

We must now return to the controversy about if, when, why and how we should ever wage war for human rights reasons. This is a debate that requires some moral, legal and also very practical consideration.

To respect the sovereignty of other nations is an obvious way of attempting to keep the peace with those powers. To obliterate this principle would be to permit or even encourage the wars of choice – including for aggression, conquest and enrichment – that have been such a recurring feature of human history. Further, the price of war can be catastrophic for the lives of millions of people, no matter how potentially noble the motives. It is far easier to destroy a civilization, no matter how imperfect or oppressive, than it is to build a new one.

Given the imperfect delivery of human rights all over the world, it could be all too easy for wars of choice to be disguised in human rights clothes, providing an alibi for all sorts of aggressors. Both Mussolini and Hitler made such spurious excuses in relation to the invasions of Ethiopia and Czechoslovakia respectively. Indeed, imperial powers and even some of their most important liberal thinkers once used the alleged barbarism of other nations to legitimize conquest.[32] Conversely of course, in the 1820s, a version of humanitarian intervention could just as easily justify British, French and Russian naval support for the war of liberation from the Ottoman Empire that was the Greek Revolution.

Acknowledging human rights foundations in internationalism and universality, it would be rather strange for a human rights advocate like me to suggest that pure self-defence is the sole ethical justification for waging war. Even criminal self-defence extends to the defence of other people. If I argue that human rights protection must know no boundaries, surely international law and international courts must sometimes be vindicated by international security – including force.

World War II began because of invasions by Axis powers. Britain entered that war because of the principle of mutual security pacts and group-based self-defence. However, it is difficult to argue, at least from a human rights perspective, that had things been different, military intervention could not have been morally justified to prevent or end the Holocaust.

Clearly, the United Nations Charter and its architecture was supposed to square this circle in 1945. It would provide balance between a respect for sovereignty as a basis of peace and interstate security, and the need for human rights protections to protect the security of vulnerable people within those same states. The Security Council was charged with a global 'policing' role in relation to the aggression of others. However, through a twenty-first-century lens, the vetoes of its permanent members begin to resemble a near-fatal flaw. Neither peace nor protection is anywhere near achieved.

Could a humanitarian intervention without Security Council authority ever be morally justified? From a human rights perspective, I would have to say, yes. The possibility of grave human rights abuses and even genocide perpetrated by permanent members or their close allies is all too real. However, this moral consideration very quickly bleeds into the practical and legal problems of unilateralism in internationalism's name. When? How? With whose authority are such self-styled humanitarian interventions to be justified in a manner that does not completely delegitimize both human rights and the wider rules-based order?

The UK Government is somewhat of an outlier in even recognizing a legal basis for such missions. This must come from a rather creative interpretation of the Charter, or bold assertion that, even outside the Charter and the UN, an embryonic 'responsibility to protect' has acquired a free-standing status under customary international law. However, it does nonetheless set itself a three-fold test for such action:

1. There is convincing evidence, generally accepted by the international community as a whole, of extreme humanitarian distress, on a large scale, requiring immediate and urgent relief;
2. It must be objectively clear that there is no practicable alternative to the use of force if lives are to be saved; and
3. The proposed use of the force must be necessary and proportionate to the aim of relief of humanitarian need and must be strictly limited in time and scope to this aim (i.e. the minimum necessary to achieve that end and for no other purpose).[33]

I do not take the view that the UK met even its own test before participating in trilateral air strikes on Syria in 2018. Further, it is perhaps beyond irony that the UK Government is currently seeking to prevent the arrival of refugees from that very conflict into its own territory. It is yet another case of using rights as justification for war over there, but not refugee protection over here. However, the ethical dilemma in the face of genocide or other human rights catastrophes and UN deadlock remains. A possible solution may lie in the institution's own history.

Uniting for Peace

This was the term used for a procedure employed by the United Nations in 1950. The context was Security Council deadlock over the Korean War. In the face of a Russian veto, the US initiated a General Assembly resolution that if the Security Council:

> because of lack of unanimity of the permanent members, fails to exercise its primary responsibility for the maintenance of international peace and security . . . the General Assembly shall consider the matter immediately.

Thus, a majority of world nations might authorize action where the old big five failed to agree.

The approach has also been used subsequently in the context of US vetoes over Israel and Palestine, so it cannot be regarded as an inherently American or partisan device. It could potentially bridge the gap between those calling for unilateral humanitarian intervention and those seeking to preserve the international rule of law. A General Assembly majority would not trump the Security Council for the purposes of the Charter. However, it would carry a great deal of legitimacy and be a basis for UN reform or the further development of customary law. Even without or before military action, it could put pressure on a recalcitrant vetoing power, and on the state perpetrating the abuse.

War is a perennial evil, the avoidance of which formed a major motivation for the new global rule of law settlement following 1945. It is always a human rights disaster and sometimes a 'state of exception' justifying temporary derogation from certain fundamental freedoms to the extent that it is 'strictly necessary'.

However, armed conflict is not a law-free zone, especially in an age of ever-more devastating threats to people and planet. Human rights principles are capable of becoming more important than ever in taming belligerents, their proxies and profiteers. They will also continue to guide and inspire those who seek to build nations and peace.

7.
Burning Injustice

Our house is on fire.

Greta Thunberg[1]

It is time to consider how human rights may contribute to the burning question facing our world, or what legendary naturalist and broadcaster Sir David Attenborough has called 'humanity's greatest threat in thousands of years'.[2]

This is not the place nor I the best advocate to persuade those of you who still do not believe climate change to be real, human-made and an emergency.[3] I write this acknowledging the possibility that you do not believe that industrialization has led to an ever-increasing volume of greenhouse gases, including carbon dioxide, to be emitted into our atmosphere, that these gases retain the heat radiated by the Earth and that, as a result, our precious planet is becoming warmer and warmer. Further, you may not share the view of most scientists and states that we must limit this warming to no more than 1.5 centigrade at the most in order to avoid the dire consequences of extreme heat, drought, rain, rising sea levels, disruption of ecosystems and food supply for our human race.

Perhaps you have not noticed unseasonal or extreme weather conditions or the unusual absence of once familiar flora and fauna where you live or around the world. In the United States alone, there were eighteen climate-related disasters in 2022. Storms, floods, wildfires and droughts caused $165 billion-worth of damage.[4] More than half of us depend on rice, maize and wheat as staple foods, and as 40 per cent of plants are under threat, so is our food security.[5] Varieties of frogs, coral, pikas (rabbit-like creatures), penguins, turtles, cod, butterflies, seals, and both the koala and polar bear are now vulnerable to extinction.

If you are in the minority, one of those who believe global warming to be natural or exaggerated in the threat that it poses, for present purposes you need merely accept the scale of contrary consensus and likely consequential political and legal developments.

A 2021 United Nations survey involving fifty countries and 1.2 million participants found that 64 per cent believed in the emergency that has now been officially declared by eighteen countries and the European Union. Over 2,300 local jurisdictions in forty countries, including those covering 95 per cent of the United Kingdom, have made similar declarations, many of which include some kind of process for action and reporting. The Paris Agreement of 2015 was the world's first globally binding, if far from perfect, climate treaty. It seeks to limit warming to 1.5 degrees, or well below 2 degrees above pre-industrial levels, by 2030. The UN Intergovernmental Panel on Climate Change (IPCC) was created as long ago as 1988 to assess the relevant science. It consistently points to the burning of fossil fuels as the number one cause of the crisis.[6]

Foundations on Fire

Some people find their own mortality hard enough to conceive. The premature extinction of life as we know it is even harder to contemplate. Desertification will leave plenty of sand in which to bury heads or vested interests. However, like it or not, this issue will increasingly dominate the remainder of most of our lives as interested citizens in what UN Secretary-General António Guterres calls 'the era of global boiling'.[7]

So the implications for rights and freedoms are worthy of discussion. Civil and political, socio-economic and cultural rights are all impacted and likely to be more so by both the worsening crisis and the responses to it. Our human rights values might help shape our laws and especially our politics in search of the 'just transition' essential to a more sustainable future. It is some of these challenges and opportunities that I want to explore.

Whether you believe that fundamental rights are somehow natural, sacred and innate, or invented necessities devised to sustain peace and progress, or, as I do, some combination of both, it is not hard to see how the worsening climate crisis, its causes and consequences must engage them. Before even considering just some of the very many individual rights in play, it is important to remember their underlying foundation in dignity, equality, fairness and universality, plus the primary recognition in the Universal Declaration that 'if man is not to be compelled to have recourse, as a last resort, to rebellion', these must be protected by the rule of law.

We face a truly global emergency on an unprecedented scale for which national sovereignty, let alone nationalistic selfishness, is particularly ill-equipped. This is combined with profound moral questions about intergenerational justice and festering historical inequities, including the costs borne by those most affected versus those most responsible for the harm.

I will leave philosophers to explain and argue about whether we owe anything on a scale from bare existence to positive flourishing to future generations.[8] A newborn infant born anywhere in the world *today* has human rights from their first breath. This alone should be enough for the current cohort of adults to feel obliged to act.

Similarly, I can leave historians and diplomats to contest the justification and viability of formal reparations for past imperial oppression. A great many people in developing countries are most affected by and least able to protect themselves from what is happening now, let alone what lies ahead. Their human rights and the planet's interconnection should be enough to justify greater and more binding burden-sharing bolstered by states with the broadest shoulders.[9]

Simmering Architecture

All major United Nations bodies, and, crucially, the Human Rights Council, High Commissioner for Human Rights and World Health Organization as well as the IPCC, acknowledge the impact of climate change upon rights to life, self-determination, health, food, water and sanitation, adequate housing and cultural rights in particular. The disproportionate vulnerability of children, women and disabled and indigenous people throw their specific treaty protections into peril. Inevitably, the framework of the Refugee Convention, already strained by rising nationalism and forced migration caused by internal and international conflict and persecution, will struggle to embrace and adequately protect those displaced by climate catastrophe.

In 2018, the UN Human Rights Committee, with its responsibility for the International Covenant on Civil and Political Rights, commented that climate change is one of 'the most pressing and serious threats to the ability of present and future generations to enjoy the right to life'.[10] It went on to pronounce on the relationship between the right to life under Article 6 of the Covenant and environmental law. So, just as there is no bright line between the laws of war and peace, we have begun to witness a vital cross-fertilization between international human rights and environmental jurisprudence designed to protect people and planet.

That rights-based conceptualization was already present in the Aarhus Convention of 1988 which came into force in 2001. Ratified by forty-five states in Europe and Central Asia, it attempts to grant the public rights of information, participation and redress over environmental decisions. It is limited to procedure rather than outcomes, and its compliance committee makes recommendations rather than binding decisions.

Nonetheless, these procedural rights, transposed into UK law via information legislation and planning acts, have empowered local activism. One example is the Friends of the Earth-supported communities who have fought fracking applications. Hydraulic fracturing, or 'fracking', is a process for recovering gas and oil from deep shale rock via drilling and injecting water, sand and chemicals at high pressure. The associated seismic tremors and considerable water usage make it controversial in the localities affected.

Naomi Luhde-Thompson of the Rights Community Action

collective argues that rights to extract information from public authorities to participate in planning and to challenge decisions can be essential community tools for defending the environment and promoting just outcomes. Nonetheless, this campaigning faces challenges from political complacency, increasing centralization of power, and people often only reaching for their rights 'when the bulldozer arrives at the end of the road'.

Injury and death due to extreme weather events are now well documented and the WHO predicts an additional 250,000 deaths each year from malnutrition, diarrhoea and heat stress alone, between 2030 and 2050. Hence states have an obligation to take positive action to mitigate the problem, to prevent this wholly foreseeable loss of life.

The priority action is confronting our addiction to fossil fuels that account for around 70 per cent of greenhouse gases. This in turn requires accelerating the development of renewable sources of energy and mitigations, such as ending deforestation. The most vulnerable people in particular countries, and across the globe, need a great deal of additional protection from the impact of climate change. Less developed countries and small island nations require unprecedented levels of financial support to deal with loss and damage, and to adapt to the future.

However, given the continuing controversy around internationalism in general, and socio-economic rights and positive obligations in particular, it isn't hard to anticipate the enormous ideological challenges alongside the logistical ones. Indeed, every indignant objection to universalism is turbocharged in the context of this challenge that only international solidarity can address. In contrast with the interconnected climate system, states and corporations have long conquered, carved up and mined the planet independently, and in competition.

Objections to collective action and shared sacrifice may not be countered by law or even human rights thinking alone. Notwithstanding our amazing imagination and ingenuity, human beings are stubbornly bad at thinking beyond our own lifespan and visualizing exponential threats. Maybe this helps with short-term personal and emotional resilience in the face of inevitable mortality and other existential questions. However, when this Micawberish instinct is multiplied by millions in advanced and ultimately urban-led civilizations, it becomes what ecologist and author William Ophuls calls 'immoderate greatness' or the growth and expansion-hungry, environment-damaging, institutional version of hubris.[11] This leads civilizations to fail.

To exacerbate the problem further, our precious democracy, with its essential periodic cycles of campaigns and elections, may also foster the short-term view, and the ebbing and flowing of visionary commitment. Just as the constitutionalizing of civil and political rights is necessary to prevent democracies from devouring themselves, a similar approach to environmental protection will inevitably become essential to preventing us from consuming our planetary home.

In the meantime, we must believe that information, participation, empowerment and redress (all protected by civil and political rights) may nudge our democracies finally to face the music. I also believe that the law may at least evolve by negotiation and interpretation so as to assist and not hinder progress.

The Problem with Paris

We are well familiar with the weakness of global governance so rooted in national sovereignty, and keeping the powerful winners of past world conflicts at the top table. Just as the biggest players have historically been major military powers, they are also often among the biggest polluters. Once more, the system requires poachers to be gamekeepers, and allows the prescribing pen to be held by some of those with the greatest incentives to prefer weaker medicine. China's annual carbon emissions have now surpassed those of the US. Its increasing influence over many developing nations creates a challenge for human rights and climate protection alike.

Indian jurist Lavanya Rajamani is Professor of International Environmental Law at the University of Oxford. She is devastating in her critique of the limitations of even the hard-won and much-prized 2015 Paris Agreement.[12]

Pointing to the underlying geopolitics, she reminds us of significant non-cooperation, even since the earlier Kyoto Protocol in 1997, by the US (under Presidents Bush and Trump), Australia (under its more right-wing governments) and Brazil (under President Bolsonaro). Paris itself allows states individually to determine their own targets for reducing emissions and creates no individual binding obligations, let alone sanctions, in relation to meeting even these. The regime lacks a sense of international or historical fairness, given that some of the greatest industrial polluters since 1850 are both most enriched and least affected by their damage. Further, there is no system for accountability in relation to the mismatch between promises made and outcomes delivered.

As we saw in the case of new technology, international treaty law has failed to keep pace adequately with the science and, as in the context of peace and security, with all too real and ever-multiplying threats. What about further legal developments outside the conference rooms and inside the courts of the world?

A new generation of climate rights lawyers has emerged with an international focus schooled by the historical hard knocks of human rights litigation and campaigning. With their comfort with comparative law from around the world, they bring an eye for using a combination of tort, constitutional, climate and human rights law, and a subtlety of understanding around the strengths and limits of strategic litigation within a wider theory of change.[13]

Climate Rights Defenders

Tessa Khan is a perfect example. Born in the UK to Bangladeshi parents in 1983, she moved first to Singapore, and then Australia as a child. After qualifying as a lawyer there, she returned to the UK for postgraduate study in Oxford before practising in The Hague, Washington DC and Thailand. She returned to the UK in 2019, and described her motivations as follows:

> In 2013, just after I'd moved to Thailand, Typhoon Haiyan, one of the most powerful tropical cyclones ever recorded, made landfall in the Philippines, killing thousands and displacing millions. It was a terrifying preview of the increasingly intense extreme weather that we can expect in a warming world, not least of all in Bangladesh, where much of my family remains. Moreover, I was conscious of the deep

> injustice of the worst impacts of climate change being visited upon the countries and communities who have done the least to contribute to the soaring concentration of greenhouse gases in our atmosphere.[14]

Inspired by the 2015 Paris Agreement, and having worked on a landmark Dutch legal case that first hit the headlines that same year, Khan collaborated with others internationally to form the Climate Litigation Network, supporting a proliferation of climate cases over the subsequent five years. *Urgenda v Netherlands*[15] had been the first case in the world in which citizens established that their government had a legal duty to prevent dangerous climate change. The non-profit NGO brought the case on behalf of 886 Dutch citizens and argued that their government had a duty to reduce Dutch emissions by 25 per cent compared to 1990. This obligation came from a combination of the Dutch civil code, Articles 2 and 8 (rights to life and to private and family life), of the European Convention on Human Rights and the 1994 UN Framework Convention on Climate Change.

In 2015, Urgenda won at first instance in the District Court of The Hague. The Dutch government appealed unsuccessfully, first to the Court of Appeal and then ultimately to the Supreme Court. Crucially, the government's contentions that its warm words and less onerous targets around emission reductions were sufficient to restrain the law from interfering in such political territory were roundly rejected by the Netherlands' highest court. The fact that the country is a former imperial and historically fossil fuel-enriched nation within the Council of Europe and ECHR system made the clear and powerful judgement even more significant internationally.

The Court agreed with both Urgenda and the Dutch government on the factual scientific consensus around the climate threat. It found that Articles 2 and 8 of the ECHR, while not imposing impossible or disproportionate burdens on the state, required suitable measures to avert the imminent hazards to life as much as reasonably possible.

It further found that the obligation to provide an effective remedy for human rights under Article 13 of the Convention meant that national courts must be able to provide effective legal protection. This, combined with the Netherlands' participation in the UN Framework Convention, created positive obligations to do its fair share in reducing emissions proportionate to its responsibility.

Most dramatically, the Supreme Court used the international consensus that developed countries (listed in Annex I to the Paris Agreement) must reduce their emissions by 25–40 per cent in 2020 to impose this as a *specific* and *binding* legal obligation on the Dutch government. Thus, as previously in our human rights history, in the absence of an international court, negotiators or legislators able to do so, a national court gave our embryonic international human rights law its teeth.

The case has to date inspired a great many climate-related cases across different jurisdictions around the world, relying on similar combinations of tort, domestic constitutional, human rights, international climate obligations and domestic targets. Young, indigenous and farming people and NGOs are often the claimants. Many have been successful, including on appeal in national supreme courts. Many more are pending at the time of writing, including five state suits, and a federal constitutional claim in the United States.[16]

A more detailed reading of just some of these claims

demonstrates the way in which even the so-called soft law of guidance and targets, whether set at the international or more domestic and local level, may harden like concrete when combined with human rights and other binding legal rules. Nonetheless, this approach is both slower and patchier than that of firm international conventions, domestic constitutions and statutes once agreed.

However, one case was special. In May 2019, a group of eight people from the Torres Strait Islands filed a complaint against the Australian government at the UN Human Rights Committee in Geneva, arguing that the country's failures to address climate change were violating their fundamental rights under the International Covenant on Civil and Political Rights. The low-lying islands are already suffering higher tides each year, coastal erosion, the regular flooding of land and homes, and reduction in traditional food supply from fishing and harvests. Rising sea temperatures are affecting the marine environment by way of coral bleaching and ocean acidification. The islanders anticipate forced displacement from their home in the near future without urgent and adequate preventative measures.

The complaint cited Articles 2 (discrimination), 6 (the right to life), 17 (the right against arbitrary interference with private and family life and home), 24 (the rights of the child) and 27 (the right to indigenous culture). The islanders argued that these had been violated by Australia's insufficient greenhouse gas targets and plans, and its failure to fund adequate coastal defence and resilience measures, such as sea walls for the islands. They fear catastrophic climate change and the total submerging of their ancestral homelands.

In September 2022, the eighteen-person Committee found that climate change was impacting the claimants' daily lives and that the Australian government's failure to secure their continued existence on the islands constituted breaches of their rights to family life and culture. A minority also found a violation of their right to life. Crucially, the Committee ordered compensation, and that steps be taken to reduce Australian emissions as fast as possible. It further ordered adequate adaptation measures in consultation with the Torres Strait Islanders.

The binding decision in international law achieved a number of landmarks in being the first by low-lying islanders against a national state, and the first time that an international tribunal has found that a country has violated human rights law via its greenhouse gas emissions and inadequate climate protection policy. It is also the first time that the right to culture has been successfully asserted in relation to climate impact. The Committee itself acknowledged the importance of its findings:

> This decision marks a significant development as the Committee has created a pathway for individuals to assert claims where national systems have failed to take appropriate measures to protect those most vulnerable to the negative impacts of climate change on the environment of their human rights.[17]

Despite such legal highs, there are few who believe that climate catastrophe may be averted by litigation alone. A particularly glaring and persistent problem remains in the form of multinational fossil fuel corporations. They enjoy limitless litigation and PR budgets facilitated by the greed of their directors, shareholders, and, it has to be conceded if only in whispers, by their lawyers. We now know, for example, that internal research by oil giants revealed the problem with carbon emissions and global warming from at least the 1970s. Nonetheless, long beyond this period, their senior executives dismissed similar scientific predictions in the public square.[18]

The plight of the Niger Delta in Nigeria demonstrates some of the consequences of this kind of grand historic corporate deception and ongoing plunder.[19] Shell personnel arrived in Ogale in the 1950s and struck black liquid gold in the form of crude oil. However, there have been continuing spills which the company consistently blames on the theft, illegal refining and sabotage of others. Damaging changes to the environment were noticed by the local community very early on.

By the 1970s, this was translating into increased human foetal abnormalities and a rise in stillbirths. In 2015, local people filed a claim against Royal Dutch Shell in London, one of the two places where Shell is incorporated. However, it took five years just to establish the competence of the UK courts to deal with claims arising from the mining activities in Nigeria.[20]

It is an interesting moral position, to say the least, to argue that you may take advantage of the attractive corporation laws and tax regimes of one country and the natural resources of another, but that you should not be held liable in the former for your allegedly illegal and certainly environmentally damaging activities in the latter. It is not a world away from past arguments by developed democracies that their prevailing rights law should in no way apply to their military adventures overseas.

Shell used the same tactical high jinks against a similar claim in the Netherlands over a Niger Delta oil spill in 2004. It took thirteen years for the four claimants to be vindicated in The Hague Court of Appeal. By this time, three of them had died and their hometown was rendered completely contaminated and uninhabitable. We can see that the Dutch legal system is fast emerging as a world leader for landmark climate protection decisions. In 2021, The Hague District Court held that Royal Dutch Shell must reduce by at least 45 per cent its net emissions by 2030 to help meet Paris targets and limit human rights violations.[21]

Of course, Shell has appealed. The possibility of throwing endless money at procedural points and multiple appeals means that, in the absence of tough suspensive interim orders against big energy companies, they can keep drilling, mining and profiting in the meantime. Time is on their side, and against the interests of people and planet. No wonder the UK Advertising Standards Authority banned a Shell campaign around its 'low-carbon' and 'cleaner energy' initiatives – a small victory perhaps, but still a moral one.[22]

Unsurprisingly, there are continuing efforts at the UN level for what would be a groundbreaking treaty to bind multinational corporations more directly to international obligations with universal enforcement duties for all states. Without this kind of global governance and policing of the world's greatest plundering and polluting entities, it is hard to see how the Paris targets and a subsequently more sustainable planet might ever be achieved.

Dalia Palombo observes an accountability gap created by the complex structures by which multinational profit machines lack legal personality, at both national and international level.[23] The hard-edged legal responsibility (under domestic regulatory, tort and criminal law, etc.) is reserved for the single constituent companies that make up the larger corporate group, and even those that sit outside, further down the supply chain. Typically, this domestic law may be enforced only at the national level. International law, including human rights law, currently only binds states directly.

Palombo further articulates a control gap, with increasing distance between directors, shareholders and 'stakeholders' (or those affected) in relation to global enterprise. There is a separation of control, information and ownership and even potentially conflicting long- and short-term interests, between professional directors and their shareholders, and even between minority and majority shareholders. There is potentially an even bigger gap between business and wider society that is exacerbated when the former establishes effective monopolies, or becomes so global as to have workers on one continent, customers on another and shareholders everywhere.

The multinational structure may effectively divide and rule all the different categories of humans affected by it (workers, customers and shareholders) because of their conflicting interests in either decent wages, low prices or high prices. Further, the environmental interests of wider stakeholders do not even feature in the governance model. So, Palombo suggests that 'purpose' and 'do no harm' objectives in relation to people and planet be entrenched in corporate law so as to permit a role for stakeholders in internal corporate governance. In addition, she advocates greater accountability by way, for example, of regulation, and litigation from outside. Once more, a belt-and-braces approach to precious rights protection.

Others campaign for an international criminal law approach via a new crime of 'ecocide'.[24] The Stop Ecocide Foundation convened a panel of lawyers from around the world and of varying disciplines to suggest a definition for such an offence. Their – as yet unrealized – hope is that this be added to the

Rome Statute, which provides the jurisdiction of the International Criminal Court. The draft formulation was published in 2021 and defines ecocide as:

> unlawful or wanton acts committed with knowledge that there is a substantial likelihood of severe and either widespread or long-term damage to the environment being caused by those acts.[25]

Tessa Khan sees the problem as even more fundamental, requiring drastic political and economic change even more than legal drafting or negotiation:

> Courts are an essential forum for clarifying and crystallising legal obligations to address climate change; they can escalate the risks of – and sanction – inaction and create powerful narratives around responsibility for the crisis. But there is no avoiding the fact that the pace and scale of the transition that is now required (especially if it is to be a just one) cannot be achieved without a political settlement encompassing industrial, social, and economic policy and that is devised, implemented, and governed at multiple levels.[26]

Returning to the UK and 'inspired by the UK's leadership on climate change in the past', she recognized an opportunity for the former industrial empire to lead the transition away from oil and gas. She founded Uplift, a multidisciplinary campaigning organization with the ambition of ensuring that Europe's second-largest oil and gas producer, also in the top ten of states with the greatest historical responsibility for the crisis, leads the way out of it.

The Iron Lady

Khan and her colleagues may well find inspiration in a potentially surprising source. Just as US President Reagan was once a great international champion of the Refugee Convention, giving his 'I am a refugee in a crowded boat' speech at Bitburg Air Base in Germany in 1985,[27] his political admirer and then UK Prime Minister Margaret Thatcher gave an early warning on the world stage about the threat of climate change. A year after the institution of the IPCC and a year before its first assessment report, she spoke about the need for global action in a now famous 1989 speech to the UN General Assembly in New York.

> What we are now doing to the world, by degrading the land surfaces, by polluting the waters and by adding greenhouse gases to the air at an unprecedented rate – all this is new in the experience of the Earth. It is mankind and his activities which are changing the environment of our planet in damaging and dangerous ways . . .
>
> We are seeing a vast increase in the amount of carbon dioxide reaching the atmosphere. The annual increase is three billion tonnes: and half the carbon emitted since the Industrial Revolution remains in the atmosphere.
>
> At the same time as this is happening, we are seeing the destruction on a vast scale of tropical forests which are uniquely able to remove carbon dioxide from the air . . .
>
> We should always remember that free markets are a means to an end. They would defeat their object if by their output they did more damage to the quality of life through pollution than the well-being they achieve by the production of goods and services . . .

> Each country has to contribute, and those countries who are industrialised must contribute more to help those who are not.[28]

Thatcher had studied chemistry at Oxford, working briefly as a research chemist, before taking the slightly more conventional pre-political route of being called to the bar. This speech reflected both aspects of that fine education, and was directed at the challenge of climate change alone. It called for specific and binding obligations on individual states based on 'sound economics'.

Of course, whether it may be considered sound economics to close down the UK's coal mining industry without a plan for replacing the jobs on which so many communities had long depended remains a bitterly contested issue in British political history. Nonetheless, there are certainly few today who openly advocate for climate change policy that fails to address people's basic ongoing economic needs, alongside the decommissioning and replacement of harmful and unsustainable industries.

Another possible lesson from that period is the vital importance of civil rights to receive information, peacefully organize, assemble and express dissent, during periods of political polarization and profound change in particular. In the 1980s Britain of my youth, much of the most anti-protest state action was directed against striking miners and others seeking to save their collieries and coal-dependent communities.

The 'Battle of Orgreave' in 1984 was a particularly notorious violent confrontation between striking miners and police officers assembled from around the country at a steel coking plant in South Yorkshire. While most media reports blamed the miners for the violence, criminal trials for riot (an offence which attracted a maximum life sentence at the time) collapsed due to the unreliability of police testimony. In 1991, South

Yorkshire Police paid a total of £425,000 in damages to thirty-nine miners for assault, wrongful arrest, unlawful detention and malicious prosecution. In 2015, the Independent Police Complaints Commission found evidence of excessive police violence, perjury by police officers during prosecutions and cover-up of that perjury by senior officers.[29] The Orgreave Truth and Justice Campaign continues to demand a full public inquiry.[30]

In the Britain of the 2020s, there is perhaps some irony in a new generation of Conservative Ministers seeking to crush protesters for taking the opposite view to striking miners, once so understandably desperate to defend livelihoods dependent on fossil fuels.

The Enemy Within

We know that people in the embryonic environmental movement were already subject to covert surveillance and infiltration by the undercover Special Demonstration Squad of the Metropolitan Police. This was created as the Special Operations Squad in 1968 under the then Labour Government of Harold Wilson in response to anti-Vietnam War demonstrations outside the US Embassy, then in London's Grosvenor Square. By the 1980s, members of groups such as Greenpeace were a target.

Police officers were authorized to undertake the kind of espionage usually reserved for intelligence services in the face of threats to national security from foreign powers, rather than the everyday criminal investigation into specific suspected offences that is the role of domestic law enforcement. Crucially, while the UK police are normally required to obtain a magistrate's warrant before entering private premises without permission, no such judicial authorization process whatsoever was required before placing officers in people's homes, friendship circles, and beds.

Further, unlike a search or even a listening device, a human intrusion of this kind creates the opportunity for a person's behaviour to be actively manipulated towards criminality by what we sometimes call the 'agent provocateur', with their determined agenda of discrediting groups rather than neutrally investigating them. When unethical, misogynist, ill-trained and still-less supervised officers are allowed to go undercover and build their 'legends' for years on end within political civil society, the opportunities for gross abuses of power are obvious and manifold.

The 'Spycops' scandal is another low point in the chequered history of British policing. It refers to the group of undercover police officers who infiltrated even wholly peaceful campaign groups, using the identity documents of dead babies, forming intimate relationships with women to protect their aliases, and in some cases even fathering children with them.[31]

At the time of writing, the scandal is still unresolved. Through a human rights lens, we can easily see violations of rights against degrading treatment, to due process, private and family life, association and expression, and against discrimination. These have been perpetrated by the British state via the Metropolitan Police on an industrial scale, involving around 140 officers and more than 1,000 political groups over forty years.

Unsurprisingly, campaigns for racial justice and against abusive policing itself were targeted alongside environmental groups.[32] Even Doreen Lawrence, now Baroness Lawrence of Clarendon on the island of Jamaica, whose campaign for justice for her murdered son Stephen led to a rewriting of race equality law to bind public authorities in the UK, was not spared.

So, anyone wondering why there has been such a coalescence between seemingly white middle-class environmental campaigns and those for racial justice against the new anti-protest laws of recent years need look no further than their shared history of anti-civil-libertarian state abuse and oppression. Transnational bonds of family and identity are likely to strengthen such alliances between them. The Global South and island nations in particular bear the brunt of climate threats first.

In 2014, the Metropolitan Police paid £425,000 to a woman called Jacqui in an out-of-court settlement of a claim for assault, negligence, deceit and other misconduct. She had been just twenty-two at the time of her intimate relationship with a police operative called Bob Lambert who disappeared in 1987 when their son was two years old. She needed psychiatric care after eventually learning of the true identity and purposes of the man she had known as Bob Robinson. Six years later, the force made a subsequent payment to her now adult son.[33]

In 2014, the then Home Secretary (later Prime Minister) Theresa May announced the Undercover Policing Inquiry.[34] Chaired by retired judge Sir John Mitting, it published its first report in June 2023. This covered the first fourteen years of secret operations between 1968 and 1982. Sir John said that he had 'come to the firm conclusion' that the methods of the Special Demonstration Squad (approved and funded by the highest levels of government) were not justified. If there had been public knowledge of it, the unit would have been closed down.

The next report will cover the crucial period from 1983 onwards.

However, the pending inquiry did not prevent May's successor Prime Minister Boris Johnson from instituting the Covert Human Intelligence Sources (Criminal Conduct) Act 2021. For the first time in UK law, this allows undercover police officers and their 'assets' in the criminal community pre-authorization to commit criminal offences in the course of their covert operations. This 'golden ticket' comes with complete immunity from criminal prosecution thereafter.[35]

In the future, protest movements might just as easily form *against* policies aimed at greening economies all over the world. Local people may be severely affected by the building of dams, farming of wind, anti-deforestation and sustainable farming edicts, and so on. Wise governments would provide information, consultation and, where necessary, support and compensation for those most affected.

The crucial role of our civil and political rights is to guarantee peaceful dissent as an important safety valve and protector of democracy itself. It is vital that these freedoms be applied and guaranteed with an even hand and that the rule of law institutions of the police and the courts are not politicized and instrumentalized by particular industries, governments, or both.

We know that peaceful protest rights to organize and dissent are not completely unfettered. Still, governments would be sensible not to set too fixed a collision course with generally non-violent movements, including those aligned to stated ambitions and obligations of states and the international community around climate protection. Unfortunately, some already have.

In recent years, a number of international human rights monitors have reported on both increased environmental activism and robust and even repressive responses from governments around the world.[36]

We can see an increased use of detention to deter and disrupt environmental protests. In the Democratic Republic of the Congo, Mombulu Boyama Alphonse, the Chief of the Mwingi tribe, was arrested and beaten by police after a community protest against the palm oil agribusiness in September 2019. In October 2020, French protesters were arrested and prosecuted for entering the tarmac at Bordeaux-Mérignac Airport. In Kazakhstan in February 2021, activists were sentenced to administrative detention after being found guilty of unsanctioned rallies against the extraction of natural gas, and expressing associated concerns around drinking water quality. The catalogue inevitably goes on.

However, given the balancing act of proportionate interference with protest rights so as to protect the rights of others, even protesters themselves will expect and even plan for arrests after a period of disruption that an effective demonstration nearly always necessitates.

Far more draconian than proportionate arrests to prevent temporary disruption from dragging on beyond the reasonable, is the increased use of political and media vilification, excessive police force, criminalization of previously non-criminal nuisance, prosecution and lengthy incarceration. These come with far harsher and longer-term consequences for the people and societies involved.

The night of 4 September 2020 seems to have proved a particular crunch point in the relationship between the climate protection movement and authorities in the UK. When protesters from the campaign group Extinction Rebellion blockaded two printworks associated with newspapers they believed to give insufficient attention to the climate threat, the government of journalist-turned-Prime-Minister Boris Johnson called it nothing short of an attack on 'our way of life'.[37] Of course, the tactic was unlikely to endear the cause to those reporting the news, not least during the heightened anxieties of the Covid-19 pandemic at that time.

This led to significant soul-searching around the wisdom of direct action versus gentler demonstrations and, as with the campaign for women's votes over a century earlier, an eventual split between the more and less militant tendencies within the movement. However, on the government side, in a country where certain newspaper titles had long wielded significant political influence, the opportunity for capitalizing on culture war with 'eco-zealots' proved impossible to resist.[38]

In the subsequent politically volatile years, the anti-protest rhetoric of some Ministers has only been matched by successively more draconian legislation.[39] This performative political activity is despite most of the increasing arrests and prosecutions being conducted under existing laws, such as obstruction of the highway.

An ever-crowded statute book now impugns non-violent dissent including noisy protest. In an imitation of anti-terrorism law, legislation includes the potential thought crime of 'going equipped to lock on'. This may encompass being in possession of luggage straps, bicycle chains, or other equipment that the police might suspect of being protest-related.

There are supplementary stop and search powers, some not even requiring reasonable suspicion, and protest-banning orders modelled on a plethora of earlier hybrid civil-criminal injunctions, aimed at diluting due process. So the 'enemy within' mindset that inspired 'Spycops' is now enshrined in law as well as rhetoric and practice.[40]

A sad and ironic twist in this tale is the number of journalists who have been arrested and detained for many hours simply for reporting on environmental protests by groups such as Just

Stop Oil, who target road traffic and motorways in particular for significant disruption. The offence used is invariably 'conspiracy to cause a public nuisance', as some argue that merely to report on protests is to give the protagonists the 'oxygen of publicity'.

On 8 November 2022, on a footbridge over the M25 motorway encircling London, LBC reporter Charlotte Lynch was arrested, handcuffed and then held for several hours in police custody, despite her press pass and microphone with her radio station insignia.[41] Even more worryingly, it later emerged that her arrest was ordered by senior officers of Hertfordshire Police.

In response, when the controversial Public Order Act 2023 was still under consideration in the House of Lords, and with a significant majority, we were able to secure a single safeguard in the form of what is now Section 17. This prevents a police officer exercising police power for the sole purpose of preventing a person from observing or reporting on a protest. I was co-signatory with former newspaper editor and active environmentalist Baroness Boycott, former police commander Lord Paddick, and retired Supreme Court Justice Lord Hope of Craighead.

Disappointingly, when other provisions of the Public Order Act were rushed into force before King Charles's Coronation in May 2023 amid a fanfare of Home Office press releases urging the police to make full use of new powers, the protection of Section 17 was not included. For some reason, the commencement of this protection was left until just under two months later.[42]

It is likely that as the threat from climate catastrophe becomes more urgent, some demonstrators may become more militant and the wider public more concerned, if still divided about particular policies. Law must protect people and property from violence, but also safeguard peaceful dissent, free reporting and vital information. If sledgehammers are used to crack walnuts of protest and not reserved for extreme disorder, the politicization of policing and the courts risks bringing law itself into disrepute. This would be as bad for democracy as any hope of an orderly, just transition to sustainability. So, the principles of proportionality and non-discrimination must inspire our policing as much as our law. Those principles still leave plenty of scope for legitimate democratic differences and political policy debate.

I am conscious that even the phrase 'just transition' will seem like a Trojan horse to some. However, if those jealously guarding a life of unthinking exponential growth and consumption that they have known for so long find burden-sharing in carbon-cutting uncomfortable, they should imagine further challenges to the privilege some of us have hitherto taken for granted.

Rising Tide

Mass climate change-inspired and induced migration is an obvious case in point. In its 2022 report, the IPCC predicted the uprooting of 143 million people over the next thirty years. Pacific Islanders will move inland due to coastal erosion. Storms will displace tens of thousands of people within densely populated Asian countries. Desertification will cause nomadic peoples in East Africa to change migration patterns. Fishing communities in West Africa will become unsustainable as ocean acidification depletes fish stocks. Latin American droughts will cause internal and international movement. And so on.

Through a post-war lens, some of these migrations will be seen as economic in nature, and others as more desperate escapes. There will be a broad and complex spectrum from choice to compulsion, depending on how drastic are the current conditions of those in flight and how negligent, venal or actively cruel and discriminatory are the policies of responsible governments and corporations.

The 1951 Refugee Convention was framed before our understanding of the climate crisis to come. It was drafted in direct response to the post-World War II refugee crisis in Europe, and the horrific events that created it. Its later protocol rendered it both global and permanent, but a Convention Refugee is still someone outside their country with a well-founded fear of 'persecution' due to their social group. It does not address people displaced within their national borders, and in most cases it may be a stretch too far to apply the concept of persecution to those fleeing a hostile, uninhabitable or submerged natural environment as opposed to a political one.

Nor are the 1954 and 1961 Conventions on the Reduction of Statelessness much better suited to reinterpretation for the crisis when, as with the Refugee Convention, too many states are seeking to shirk, rather than expand, their existing and obvious international obligations even towards some of their own citizens. So, while the term 'climate refugee' makes sense in ordinary parlance, it has yet to acquire anything like a settled legal status for the purposes of effective human rights protection.

Ideally, and as in the face of climate catastrophe more generally, there will be new treaties creating clear and binding obligations on states and corporations in relation to both responsibility-sharing and permanent relocation for people within and across national borders.

In the meantime, the principle of non-refoulement may have to serve as first aid while we call, and wait, for more satisfactory long-term remedies. The term was first used in Article 13 of the Refugee Convention as the rule against turning away or forcing back refugees. There is similar provision in the UN Convention against Torture and other Cruel, Inhuman or Degrading Treatment or Punishment, preventing the expulsion, return ('refoulement') or extradition of people to other states where there are substantial grounds for believing them to be at grave risk.

However, it has now been used in several other treaties. Further, it is generally considered to have become part of settled customary international law not to send people to places of real risk of serious harm. This is therefore binding upon all states, regardless of the particular agreements which they have or have not ratified.

In a 2020 test case, the UN Human Rights Committee considered Ioane Teitiota's complaint against New Zealand for denying his asylum claim and returning him to Kiribati, a country made up of thirty-two small Pacific islands. The Committee recognized 'environmental degrading, climate change and unsustainable development' as serious threats to life and that those who flee natural disasters due to climate change must not be returned so as to put their lives at risk. Still, Teitiota's claim that Kiribati would be totally uninhabitable within ten to fifteen years was insufficiently imminent and there was a lack of proof that the country would not undertake sufficient adaptation measures by then. His claim was therefore denied.

The human rights clock is ticking and adjusting to this shortening fuse. It would be far better for people and planet for this crisis and the human rights challenges it throws up to be equitably and effectively resolved via global political statesmanship rather than international or even domestic courts. However, if nation states fail adequately to respond in cooperation, or on the scale required, others will no doubt do their best. Reaching out now is better than castigating others for over-reaching later on.

Conclusion

Democracy values everyone equally
even if the majority does not.

Brenda Hale[1]

I began this book while a deadly pandemic raged and finished it well over a year into a European conflict that once more threatens world security. In the interim, we have seen increased inequality and economic turmoil, accelerating threats from artificial intelligence, and dire warnings lest we miss vital global emissions targets. We face the biggest refugee crisis since just after World War II, and the biggest displacement of people in our history. Hard men dominate too many nations and corporations. Fundamental rights and freedoms seem in retreat everywhere, just when we need them the most.

I have tried to summarize a far longer, richer and more controversial story to which we can only write further chapters together. I believe we must strive to avert its ending, alongside our own. Human rights are as precious and imperfect as we are. These perhaps contradictory truths must nonetheless hold. I began my introduction with the words of a great philosopher on 'dignity', and for this conclusion, turn to a world-leading judge on the essence of 'democracy'.

These are the two continuing justifications for the origins and advancement of human rights.

Our freedoms have been paid for in centuries of courage and blood, and we have seen a historical continuum in the many people's struggles that are too rarely linked to the overall development of our modern fundamental rights. Unpicking the partial and over-edited histories that have deliberately sought to separate the hard-won liberties of different groups of formerly disempowered people reveals some authors seeking to fend off the universality of rights, and the problem it poses for the most dogmatic, and powerful, everywhere.

I have been guided and challenged by the work of some wonderful and lucid members of the international academy. Their scholarship, like humanity, knows no borders. I have also been inspired by some remarkable lawyers and campaigners, and brave and brilliant people who are neither and both.

In sketching major developments in human history and the main legal instruments that now protect us, I hope I have shown some of their value at international, regional and national levels. These have never purported to be mystical magical spells or inaccessible algorithms for problem-solving. They are vital frameworks for negotiation and adjudication, nonetheless. These must not only be known and argued about by lawyers, but owned and understood by everyone, and everywhere. Anyone who remembers the players in their favourite sports team, actors in their preferred soap opera or ingredients in their grandmother's recipe should have at least some familiarity with their basic human rights.

Our civil liberties are crucial to democracy, which isn't limited to casting a vote – if you're entitled to, at your age, and where you live – every few years. Protection from cruelty, forced labour, arbitrary detention and unfair penalties is essential to any meaningful personhood, and still not realized for so many people all over the world. Privacy and family life are subject to unprecedented threats, not least from expansive police powers and new technologies. Conscience and faith are still the subject of persecution and too many people still price their own speech and expression as free, and others' as too expensive.

The progressive development of social and economic rights is also not where it might be, over seven decades from their formal recognition. This has been set back by the pandemic and various conflicts, but also by entrenched inequality and greed. They will only be further challenged by the climate emergency, which in turn cannot be addressed without some substantial resettlement. And there can be no rights to redress or access to justice, even for civil rights, without state investment.

Cultural rights are often neglected, and yet without their protection and enjoyment, we are rendered less than human. Culture has played a significant part in our human rights story. Literature and drama allowed us to travel vast distances long before aeroplanes. They opened up channels of empathy and allowed us to identify with those we would never otherwise meet. It is no coincidence that the golden age of cinema coincides with the rise of international human rights in an optimistic moment after the privations of two, too-proximate world wars.

Visual arts and music are each as vibrant an international language as rights themselves. The recognition of cultural rights is an essential way of respecting the local as well as the universal, and of protecting precious minority traditions from erasure. Once more, these cannot be delivered without some investment by states.

National belonging can be a wonderful thing and the privileges of citizenship rightly engage certain duties in return. As a daughter of the Commonwealth and of immigrants to the United Kingdom, I have had the most fortunate of lives and try to repay the debt to others. Fortune is the right word, as it is only life's lottery that determined my time and place. I suspect that whether you believe in that lottery is a big ideological dividing line. If you think that being born in a Global North hospital to kind parents in reasonable circumstances, rather than to a dying stateless mother in a refugee camp, is a matter of character and not luck, I will have struggled to persuade you otherwise in these pages.

History shows us the ease with which both fortune and privilege may be tightly limited to those deemed worthy by those ruling nation states at certain moments. If it is hard to imagine women or people of particular ethnicity lacking freedom or equal rights, think of all the places where these have been pushed back, even in recent decades.

If it's inconceivable that a once open nation would turn on a religious, racial or sexual minority or its neighbours, think again. The limitation of even noble national identities and citizenship rights is that they may be given and taken away in almost a heartbeat by whoever is running your country in that moment. Previous generations understood this and so they distilled inalienable rights that belong to all human beings everywhere. These should protect them from abuse, or at least justify an appropriately robust response when that abuse is attempted or perpetrated.

As I hope to have shown, this idea of universality was coined long ago. Still, its infinite wisdom has become more, not less, valuable as the years have passed. Power has collected at the very top tables of the planet, but democratic governance has not, or at least not in anything approaching an equivalence capable of holding such power to account.

International solidarity in statecraft and among people has also become the only realistic way to stave off global threats and challenges, which, while mostly of our own making, may never be remotely fended off by individual nations or even small groups of them, alone.

This is true of inequality, pandemics, advanced technologies, insecurity and violent conflict, and the potential climate catastrophe that threatens our premature ending as a race. This obviously requires multilateral state cooperation, but also accountability for gross violations of human rights and other crimes, even across borders. Democratic states in particular should set an example by being more open and less defensive about mistakes and abuses of the present and the past.

Mostly this requires better leadership, but one of the tasks of that global leadership in the twenty-first century must be to reform some of our international institutions, so that they may be more trusted and effective in helping to safeguard human rights when they are under threat at regional, national and local levels.

This presents a whole range of extremely difficult dilemmas, not least sitting down with less than palatable leaders, dictators even, in pursuit of progress on people and planet. This may be done with integrity and even a degree of openness, as long as the enrichment of some is not being traded for the rights of others.

One thing that I have learned on this journey is that before even the machines and artificial intelligence that we engineered and permitted, we designed other devices capable of working against our shared human interest, if left without adequate democratic or even legal control. The weakness in global governance has been a repeated theme in my human rights investigation.

A recurring problem is multinational corporations, with their opaque and Byzantine legal structures, and the many thinking and un-thinking facilitators of these. Just as Big Tech pioneers and leaders are now openly calling for much more regulatory governance – no doubt to protect their consciences and reputations – I suspect that other sensible global industries, including law firms, may soon follow.

Rights-washing, like green-washing, diversity-washing and all the other offerings of the modern laundromat, will be insufficiently cleansing in an increasingly legally literate and curious world to which I seek to contribute. Every collective human enterprise, whether governmental, religious, charitable or profitable, will soon perhaps search its soul, practice, supply chain, clients, customers and wider social base with the care with which it curates its website. For this we must hope and actively work.

In the meantime, we should inspect the weakness of our own position with equal rigour. Universalism and greater global governance bring their own risks too. We do not aspire to a more casually dressed version of corporate globalization, but with NGOs and diplomats replacing the imperialist commanders or money men of the past and present. Human rights have to be as rooted in local communities as in international treaties, if they are to offer anything real and relevant to those they were fashioned to protect.

Civil and political, and cultural rights in particular, were framed to recognize that one size cannot fit all, even in the context of equal dignity and worth. We yearn for our own particular cultures, politics, faith, languages and expression, our right to be different, even wrong in the eyes of others. And well we might.

So whatever the ground rules and wisdom of referees, democratic leadership must still be won at the ballot box. This is why our human rights are not just for lawyers and judges, and why lawyers and judges must safeguard democracy with a humility that never seeks to usurp it. A delicate reciprocity requires that even elected leaders with huge popular support should be accountable to law, and that the law gives appropriate respect to reasonable democratic choices and decisions, taken with due care and consideration, including for human rights.

If you are now rolling your eyes, I am grateful that you have stuck with me for this long. If I have sometimes sounded political, that is because I am an openly political person, but I have tried to distinguish between hard legal obligations and moral and political choices. That said, I believe that democratic politics of different persuasions may be as informed by human rights values and principles as our laws. The value of human dignity is a case in point, as are the principles of proportionality, equal treatment, and many more. Our human rights framework was agreed and developed by people from across the democratic spectrum over the centuries. I have tried to suggest how it might inspire rather than irritate them today.

I believe in the famous 'close to home' argument. This means that even as individuals, in our homes, schools, workplaces and communities, we may try to practise what we preach when it comes to human rights in particular. We can avoid cruelty and denigration of others, whether on or offline, no matter how much we disagree with them.

We can seek to protect colleagues at work, including by joining and facilitating trade unions. We can be the consumers who, subject to our means, have a thought for where that product came from, the human and environmental conditions under which it was made, and where the packaging and waste will end up. We can try to be fair and proportionate in our dealings with and judgements of others. We can challenge our own prejudices every day.

If this seems too saccharine, wait for the twist. I also believe we have an obligation to stand up for human rights, especially those of others, and the most vulnerable in particular. Sometimes this takes courage. It isn't always fashionable and being outside a cheering or baying crowd can often feel uncomfortable. These rights aren't there to make us comfortable. They exist to keep us free.

Acknowledgements

I am so grateful to my wonderful Wylie Agents Sarah Chalfant, Emma Smith and Samuel Sheldon for unerring advice, belief and care.

I thank my Penguin publishers Maria Bedford, Sandra Fuller, Rebecca Lee, Stuart Proffitt, Alice Skinner, Noosha Alai-South, Ingrid Matts, Gavin Read, Thi Dinh, and Maddie Watts for variously commissioning, editing, producing, and championing this work.

Tamsin Shelton's meticulous close eye and copy-editing, Olga Kominek's beautiful jacket and Mark Wells' index have been an enormous privilege.

My dear first readers and discussants were Ellie Hobhouse, Rachel Holmes, MairiClare Rodgers, Tyrone Steele, and Marypaz Arrieta-Ventura. Their patience was heroic and support completely priceless.

Some of the greatest expert brains are also the most generous:

Duncan Bell, University of Cambridge, Silkie Carlo, Big Brother Watch, Anjali Mazumder, Alan Turing Institute, John Tasioulas and Michael Wooldridge, University of Oxford (Chapter 5), Nicholas Mercer, formerly of the British Army and Ann Grant, formerly of the United Kingdom Foreign and Commonwealth Office (Chapter 6), Linda Lakhdhir, Climate Rights International, Tessa Khan, Uplift, Randeep Ramesh, The Guardian and Naomi Luhde-Thompson, Rights Community Action (Chapter 7), Dalia Palombo, University of Tilburg (Chapters 5,6, and 7), Andrea Coomber, formerly of JUSTICE and now of The Howard League for Penal Reform, and UN Independent Expert Graeme Reid, formerly of Human Rights Watch. Unattributed opinions and any errors are obviously mine alone.

Inspiration, solidarity, and precious advice of so many kinds came from: Rose Amaral, Biddy Arnott, Zoe Bantleman, Lucy Blair, Christine Blower, Sue Bowyer, Pauline Bryan, Florri Burton, Michael Cashman, Polly Clayden, Nic Clements, Liam Collins, Dana Denis-Smith, Baljit Dhadda, Catherine Dobson, the late Murray Elder, Dave Ernshaw, Stephanie Harrison, Miranda and the Havelock Allans, John Hendy, David Herd, Raza Hussain, Brian Leveson, Becky Long-Bailey, Stella and Toby Low, Nick Manners, Fiona Macdonald, Rosamond McDowell, Sadie Morgan, Sonali Naik, Alice Pearson, Anna Pincus, Deok Joo Rhee, Gary Rokenson, Bell Ribeiro-Addy, Jane Samuels, Emeli Sandé, Isabella Savill, Amrit Singh, Liz Symons, Rachel Wainwright, Kirsty Warner, Libby Watkins, Harriet and Vanessa Wheldon, Peter York, and Lea Ypi.

For the best view and warmest retreat, I cannot give enough thanks to: Aidan, Angus, Beth, Carl, Caroline, Charlotte, Chloe, Daniel, Elyssia, Emma, Eve, Finlay, Gavin, Izzy, Johnny, Keira, Kian, Lucy, Megan, Michelle, Michael, Molly, Nicky, Olivia, Sally, Scarlett, and Sean.

In my current place of learning, I've benefited from debates and discussions with: Ros Altmann, David Alton, David Anderson, Willie Bach, Natalie Bennett, David Blunkett, Paul Boateng, Rosie Boycott, Des Browne, Deborah Bull, Alex Carlisle, Ken Clarke, Vernon Coaker, Ray Collins, Patrick Cormack, Jack Cunningham, Rita Donaghy, Alf Dubs, Terence Etherton, Charlie Falconer, Anita Gale, Mary Goudie, Leslie Griffiths, John Gummer, Peter Hain, Sally Hamwee, Richard Harries, Arminka Helic, David Hope, Jenny Jones, Roy Kennedy, Beeban

Kidron, Timothy Kirkhope, Ruth Lister, Sarah Ludford, Molly Meacher, Nosheena Mobarik, the late and learned John Morris, Nuala O'Loan, Onora O'Neill, Brian Paddick, Chris Patten, Dawn Primarolo, Tim Razzall, John Reid, Margaret Ritchie, Jeff Rooker, Simon Russell, Liz Sanderson, Fiona Shackleton, Kevin Shinkwin, Elizabeth Butler-Sloss, Liz Sugg, Glenys Thornton, Fiona Twycross, Alan West, Sayeeda Warsi, Simon Woolley and many others.

The late and learned Igor Judge was such a close reader of my earlier books. I shall miss his thoughts on this one and a great deal else.

To the late and learned Simon Brown, I owe so much gratitude and respect for decades of friendship and a lifetime of public service.

This book is in memory of my parents whose values helped shape my own.

Notes

Introduction

1 Ronald Dworkin, *Justice for Hedgehogs* (Harvard University Press, 2011), pp.422–3.
2 Eleanor Roosevelt, 'The Great Question', speech to the United Nations in New York, 27 March 1958.

1. Foundations

1 Toni Morrison, *Barnard Commencement Speech*, 1979.
2 George Santayana, *Reason in Common Sense* (Constable, 1905).
3 Lynn Hunt and Samuel Moyn are two of the most compelling exponents of the first and second approaches. See e.g. *Inventing Human Rights* (W.W. Norton and Co., 2007) and *Human Rights and the Uses of History* (Verso, 2017).
4 See Ronald Dworkin's masterwork *Justice for Hedgehogs*.
5 Ibid., pp.422, 423.
6 Tom Bingham, *The Rule of Law* (Penguin Allen Lane, 2010).
7 Aristotle, *Nicomachean Ethics*, trans. J. A. K. Thomson (Penguin Books, 1955), Book 5, Ch. 7.
8 Thomas Aquinas, *Summa Theologica* (Leonine Commission, Rome, 1882–1948).
9 *The Rule of Law*, p.10.
10 *Bushell's Case* (1670) 124 E.R. 1006.
11 *The Rule of Law*, p.14.

12 See e.g. Blackstone and Coke.

13 The 'nom de plume' of French Enlightenment writer and polymath François-Marie Arouet. See e.g. Voltaire, *Letters on England*, 1733 (Penguin Classics, 1980), Ken Armstrong, 'Broken on the Wheel', *The Paris Review*, 13 March 2005.

14 *Inventing Human Rights*, p.76.

15 Ibid., p.81.

16 *Human Rights and the Uses of History*, Ch. 8.

17 Shami Chakrabarti, *On Liberty* (Penguin Allen Lane, 2014), p.97.

18 Hugo Grotius, *De Jure Praedae Commentarius*, Prolegomena.

19 See Thomas Paine, *Common Sense* (1766) and *Rights of Man* (1790).

20 From the Preamble to the Declaration of Independence, 1776.

21 *Inventing Human Rights*, p.16.

22 These arguments were overruled by the Supreme Court in *New York State Rifle and Pistol Association v Bruen*, 597 U.S. (2022).

23 Jenny S. Martinez, *The Slave Trade and the Origins of International Human Rights Law* (Oxford University Press, 2012).

24 Ibid., p.6.

25 As under Roman law.

26 John Locke, *Second Treatise of Government*, 1689 (Cambridge University Press, 1988), Ch. 4, 'Of Slavery'.

27 Jean-Jacques Rousseau, *The Social Contract*, 1788 (Penguin, 2005).

28 See e.g. non-binding 'obiter dictum' comments of Lord Henley, 1st Earl of Northington and Lord High Chancellor, in *Shanley v Harvey* (1763) 2 Eden 126.

29 *Somerset v Stewart* (1772) 98 ER 499.

30 Mary Wollstonecraft, *A Vindication of the Rights of Woman*, 1792 (Penguin Classics, 2004).

31 Ibid., Part 1, Ch. 2.

32 See in particular Rachel Holmes, *Sylvia Pankhurst: Natural Born Rebel* (Bloomsbury, 2021) for arguments for and against universalism within the suffragette movement.

33 See e.g. US Supreme Court decisions in *Griswold v Connecticut*, 381 U.S. 479 (1965) on birth control, and *Roe v Wade*, 410 U.S. 113 (1973) on abortion – overturned by *Dobbs v Jackson Women's Health Organization*, 597 U.S. (2022), and Shami Chakrabarti, *Of Women* (Penguin Allen Lane, 2017).

34 See e.g. *Thlimmenos v Greece*, App. no. 3469/97, ECHR, 6 April 2000.

35 See in particular H. G. Wells, *The Rights of Man*, 1940 (Penguin, 2015 Edition with foreword by Ali Smith).

36 See e.g. Martin Gilbert, *The Holocaust: A History of the Jews of Europe during the Second World War* (Henry Holt and Company, 1985), p.485.

37 Drafted during the war, signed in June 1945, and effective from 24 October that year.

38 The French Civil Code, 'Code civil', established in 1804, much amended and still in force. Prioritizing clear and accessible law over previous patchworks, it has been hugely significant in emerging legal systems internationally, not least in Latin America and the Middle East.

39 *The Autobiography of Eleanor Roosevelt*, 1961 (Zed, 2018 Edition).

40 Confucianism describes the philosophy, tradition or religion springing from the teachings of the Chinese philosopher Confucius (551–479 BCE).

41 'Apartheid' ('separateness' in Afrikaans) was a system of institutionalized and white supremacist racial segregation, stratification and oppression in South and South West Africa from 1948 to the early 1990s.

2. Architecture

1 'Law Like Love', 1939, *W. H. Auden: Selected Poems*, edited by Edward Mendelson (Faber & Faber, 2010).

2 ICESCR, Articles 6 and 7.
3 Ibid., Article 8.
4 Ibid., Articles 9 and 10.
5 Ibid., Article 11.
6 Ibid., Article 12.
7 Ibid., Articles 13 and 14.
8 Ibid., Article 15.
9 ICCPR, Article 3.
10 Ibid., Article 4.
11 Ibid., Articles 7 and 8.
12 Ibid., Article 9.
13 Ibid., Article 10.
14 Ibid., Article 11.
15 Ibid., Articles 12 and 13.
16 Ibid., Articles 14 and 15.
17 *R v R* [1991] UKHL 12.
18 ICCPR, Articles 16 and 17.
19 Ibid., Article 18.
20 Ibid., Article 19.
21 Ibid., Article 20.
22 'Down by the Riverside'/'Study War No More' is a famous African-American spiritual and anti-war song.
23 See Articles 2(4) and 51 of the United Nations Charter 1945 and Chapter 6 to come.
24 ICCPR, Articles 21, 22, 23 and 24.
25 Ibid., Article 25.
26 Ibid., Article 26.
27 Ibid., Article 27.
28 Belgium, Denmark, France, Ireland, Italy, Luxembourg, the Netherlands, Norway, Sweden and the United Kingdom signed the Treaty of London at the outset in May 1948. Turkey and Greece joined three months later.

29 See David Weissbrodt and Cheryl Heilman, 'Defining Torture, Cruel, Inhuman, and Degrading Treatment', *Law and Inequality*, 29, 343, 2011, available at https://scholarship.law.umn.edu/faculty_articles/366.
30 *Miller v California*, 413 U.S. 15 (1973).
31 *Brandenburg v Ohio*, 395 U.S. 444 (1969).
32 *Harper & Row v Nation Enterprises*, U.S. 539 (1985).
33 The Human Rights Act 1998, c.42.
34 The Illegal Migration Act 2023, c.37.
35 ECHR, Article 1, Protocol 1.
36 Ibid., Article 2, Protocol 1.
37 Ibid., Article 3, Protocol 1.
38 With a membership of 55 states and founded in 2001 in Addis Ababa, Ethiopia.
39 ACHPR, Article 19.
40 Ibid., Article 20.
41 Ibid., Article 21.
42 Ibid., Article 22.
43 Ibid., Article 23.
44 Ibid., Article 24.

3. *Trojan Horse or Human Shield?*

1 In the second book of the *Aeneid* by Virgil, Greek soldiers infiltrate and subsequently sack the fortified city of Troy by hiding inside a giant wooden horse from which they emerge after nightfall.
2 See e.g. commentary around the US Former Secretary of State Mike Pompeo's Commission on Unalienable Rights (2019) and the aborted UK Bill of Rights Bill (2022).
3 'The Judge Over Your Shoulder' is a now legendary guidance document for UK Government officials the first edition of which was published in 1987.

4 See e.g. Debora Mackenzie, 'The Covid-19 Pandemic was predicted – here's how to stop the next one', *New Scientist*, 16 September 2020.

5 Shami Chakrabarti, 'After the Sarah Everard vigil scandal, who still thinks the police need extra powers?', *the Guardian*, 14 March 2021.

6 'Bodies of Covid-19 victims among those dumped in Ganga river: Govt', *Hindustan Times*, 16 May 2021.

7 Bhargav Acharya, 'UK to receive 10 million AstraZeneca COVID-19 vaccine doses from India's Serum Institute', *Reuters*, 3 March 2021.

8 See in particular Sarah E. Boslaugh, *Health Care Systems Around the World: A Comparative Guide* (Sage Publications, 2013).

9 See Matthew Desmond, *Poverty, by America* (Penguin, 2023).

10 See Hettie O'Brien, 'Private Equity has its sights on the NHS', *the Guardian*, 17 August 2023.

11 'Care and Support Reimagined: A National Care Covenant for England', churchofengland.org

12 Figures and analysis from nokidhungry.org

13 Foodfoundation.org.uk

14 See e.g. Salar Mohandesi, *Red Internationalism: Anti-Imperialism and Human Rights in the Global Sixties and Seventies* (Cambridge University Press, 2023).

15 See e.g. Jessica Whyte, *The Morals of the Market: Human Rights and the Rise of Neoliberalism* (Verso, 2019).

16 See e.g. Robert Verkaik, 'The super-rich are trying to exploit human rights law to dodge tax', *the Guardian*, 16 November 2017.

17 Italicized for my emphasis.

18 For a short and accessible analysis of some of the arguments around corporate human rights, see Andreas Kulick, 'Corporate Human Rights?', Faculty of Law Blogs, University of Oxford, 22 December 2020.

19 See e.g. Rwanda Radio Transcripts, translated and curated by the Montreal Institute for Genocide and Human Rights Studies at Concordia University, Concordia.ca

4. *When Rights Clash*

1 'The Colossus', Sylvia Plath, *The Colossus and Other Poems*, 1960 (Faber & Faber, 2008).
2 See e.g. James Griffin, *On Human Rights* (Oxford University Press, 2008).
3 Ibid.
4 *R v SSHD, Ex parte Limbuela and Ors*, House of Lords, 2005.
5 *R vSSSS, Ex parte B and Joint Council for the Welfare of Immigrants*, CA, 21 June 1996.
6 *A v UK*, App. no, 25599/94, ECHR, 1998.
7 *S.W. v UK*, App. no. 20166/92, ECHR, 1995.
8 See Justice O. Douglas in *Griswold v Connecticut*, 381 U.S. 479 (1965). Privacy rights read into 3rd Amendment protection of the home, 4th Amendment protection from unreasonable searches, 5th Amendment protection from self-incrimination and 9th Amendment protection of other retained rights.
9 See *Campbell v MGN* [2004] 2AC 457.
10 Ibid.
11 *Peck v UK*, App. no. 4467/98, ECHR, 2003.
12 *Venables v News Group Newspapers Ltd, Thompson v News Group Newspapers Ltd* [2001] EWHC QB 32.
13 See *Goodwin v UK*, App. no. 28957/95, ECHR, 2002.
14 In the 2002 Declaration of Principles for Freedom of Expression in Africa.
15 See *Lee v Ashers Baking Company Ltd and Ors* [2018] UKSC 49.

16 For a rehearsal of some of the arguments, see *Masterpiece Cakeshop v Colorado Civil Rights Commission*, 584 U.S. (2028).

17 E.g. Zimbabwe, Kenya and South Africa.

18 For an innovative example, see Ndjodi Ndeunyema, *Re-invigorating Ubuntu through Water: A Human Right to Water under the Namibian Constitution* (Pretoria University Law Press, 2021).

19 Chris Wrigley, 'Churchill and the Trade Unions', *Transactions of the Royal Historical Society*, Vol. 11 (Cambridge University Press, 2001), pp. 273–93.

5. Modern Prometheus

1 Mary Shelley, *Frankenstein; or, The Modern Prometheus*, 1818 (Penguin Classics, 2003).

2 The Destruction of Stocking Frames, etc. Act 1812 (c.16), also known as The Frame-Breaking Act.

3 See Gerard DeGroot, *The Bomb: A Life* (Harvard University Press, 2005).

4 Atomicarchive.com

5 Linus Pauling, 'Notes on Conversation with Albert Einstein', 16 November 1954. To be found at various US university archives and online.

6 Electronic Frontier Foundation, eff.org

7 Niamh Rowe, '"It's destroyed me completely": Kenyan moderators decry toll of training of AI models', *the Guardian*, 2 August 2023.

8 See e.g. 'British Businesses to Save Billions Under New UK Version of GDPR', DSIT Press Release, gov.uk, 8 March 2023.

9 'A pro-innovation approach to AI regulation', Command Paper 815, March 2023.

10 See e.g. Cathy O'Neil, *Weapons of Math Destruction* (Penguin Allen Lane, 2016).

11 Joshua Fairfield, *Runaway Technology* (Cambridge University Press, 2021).
12 *On Liberty*, Ch. 5, and Chapter 6 here.
13 See accounts of Deep Blue v Garry Kasparov (1996–97).
14 See Meredith Broussard, *More than a Glitch: Confronting Race, Gender, and Ability Bias in Tech* (MIT Press, 2023).
15 'AI has much to offer humanity. It could also wreak terrible harm', *The Observer*, 2 April 2023.
16 Safe.ai
17 Sir Arthur Conan Doyle, 'The Adventure of Silver Blaze' from *The Memoirs of Sherlock Holmes*, 1892.
18 Since the Police and Criminal Evidence Act 1984.
19 The Baroness Casey Review, met.police.uk, March 2023.
20 Evani Radiya-Dixit, 'A Sociotechnical Audit: Assessing Police Use of Facial Recognition', mctd.ac.uk, October 2022.
21 See e.g. Kashmir Hill, 'Eight Months Pregnant and Arrested After False Facial Recognition Match', *The New York Times*, 6 August 2023.
22 See Amelia Gentleman, *The Windrush Betrayal: Exposing the Hostile Environment* (Guardian Faber, 2020).
23 Ruha Benjamin, *Race After Technology* (Polity, 2019).
24 See e.g. Jonathan Steele, 'Stanislav Petrov obituary', *the Guardian*, 11 October 2017.
25 *Weapons of Math Destruction* (Penguin Allen Lane, 2016).
26 Andrew Gregory, 'AI use in breast cancer screening as good as two radiologists, study finds', *the Guardian*, 2 August 2023.
27 11 August 2023, nice.org.uk
28 See Hannah Fry, *Hello World: How to be Human in the Age of the Machine* (Black Swan, 2019), Ch. 2: Data.
29 See Dafna Dror-Shpoliansky and Yuval Shany, 'It's the End of the (Offline) World as we know it: From Human Rights to Digital Human Rights – A Proposed Typology', *European Journal of International Law*, Vol.32, no. 4, 2021.

30 Ibid.

31 See 'Ethics guidelines for trustworthy AI', April 2019, digital-strategy.ec.europa.eu. See also US President Biden's Executive Order on Safe, Secure and Trustworthy Artificial Intelligence, www.whitehouse.gov, 30 October 2023 and The Bletchley Declaration, www.gov.uk 1-2 November 2023.

6. *War and Peace*

1 Ernest Hemingway, *For Whom the Bell Tolls*, 1955 (Penguin Vintage Classics, 2022).

2 The GSS Torture Case, Supreme Court of Israel, 6 September 1999.

3 See Michael Walter, *Just and Unjust Wars: A Moral Argument with Historical Illustrations* (Basic Books, first published 1977, 5th Edition, 2015).

4 Andrew Fiala and Jennifer Kling, *Can War be Justified? A Debate* (Routledge, 2023).

5 Modern war in particular: Gerard DeGroot, *The Bomb: A Life* (Harvard University Press, 2005).

6 Siegfried Sassoon, 'Finished with the War: A Soldier's Declaration', July 1917.

7 See Oona A. Hathaway and Scott J. Shapiro, *The Internationalists and Their Plan to Outlaw War* (Penguin, 2018).

8 See the 'Torture Memos' – Memorandum Regarding Military Interrogation of Alien Unlawful Combatants Held Outside the United States, 2002.

9 George Orwell, *Politics and the English Language*, 1946, 20th Edition (Penguin Classics, 2013).

10 Thomas W. Smith, *Human Rights and War Through Civilian Eyes* (University of Pennsylvania Press, 2017).

11 Ch. V, United Nations Charter 1945.

12 *Saadoune v Russia and Ukraine* (App. no. 2844/22), *Pinner v Russia and Ukraine* (App. no. 31217/22) and *Aslin v Russia and Ukraine* (App. no. 31233/22).
13 Italicized for my emphasis.
14 *Banković and Others v Belgium*, App. no. 55721/11, ECHR, 2001.
15 *Alejandro v Cuba*, [1999] IACoHR 86/99, Case 11.589.
16 Dalia Palombo, 'Extraterritorial, Universal, or Transnational Human Rights Law?', *Israel Law Review*, Cambridge University Press (online), November 2022.
17 *Channel 4 News*, 22 January 2016.
18 Statement given to the author.
19 See *On Liberty* and *Human Rights and War Through Civilian Eyes*.
20 Ibid., p.157.
21 *Al-Skeini and Others v the UK*, App. no 55721/11, ECHR, 2011.
22 See the opinion of Judge Bonello in the above.
23 The Report of the Baha Mousa Inquiry, the Rt Hon. Sir William Gage, 2011.
24 See e.g. *Findlay v UK* (App. no. 22107/93), *Morris v UK* (App. no. 38784/97), *Boyd and Others v Army Prosecuting Authority and Others* [2002] UKHL31, *Cooper v UK* (App. no. 48843/99), *Grieves v UK* (App. no. 57067/00), *R v Stow* [2005] EWCA Crim 157.
25 Aaron Sorkin, *A Few Good Men*, Samuel French Inc, 2012.
26 *A Few Good Men*, Director, Rob Reiner, Columbia Pictures, 1992. See also *The Mauritanian*, Director, Kevin Macdonald, STX Pictures, 2021, based on *Guantánamo Diary*, Mohamedou Ould Slahi (Little, Brown, 2015).
27 Overseas Operations (Service Personnel and Veterans) Act 2021, c.23.
28 *R (Campaign Against Arms Trade) v Secretary of State for International Trade and Others* [2019] EWCA Civ 2020.
29 [2020] 37919.

30 *Estados Unidos Mexicanos v Smith & Wesson Brands Inc and Others* (2022) US District Court of Massachusetts, Case 1:21-cv-11269-FDS.
31 See e.g. Benoit Faucon, Joe Parkinson and Thomas Grove, 'Why Wagner Chief Prigozhin Turned Against Putin', *Wall Street Journal*, 27 June 2023.
32 E.g. J. S. Mill, *A Few Words on Non-intervention*, 1859.
33 'Global Britain: The Responsibility to Protect and Humanitarian Intervention: Government response to the Committee's Twelfth Report', 8 November 2018, available at https://publications.parliament.uk/pa/cm201719/cmselect/cmfaff/1719/171902.htm

7. *Burning Injustice*

1 Greta Thunberg, Speech to the World Economic Forum, Davos, January 2019.
2 At the 24th Conference of the Parties to the UN Framework Convention on Climate Change (COP24), Katowice, Poland, December 2018.
3 For the evidence, see e.g. *The Climate Book*, created by Greta Thunberg (Penguin Allen Lane, 2022), and Mark Maslin, *How to Save Our Planet: The Facts* (Penguin Life, 2021).
4 National Oceanic and Atmospheric Administration.
5 'State of the World's Plants and Fungi', Royal Botanic Gardens, Kew, 2020.
6 See e.g. IPCC, Sixth Assessment Report (AR6), 20 March 2023.
7 See e.g. Ajit Niranjan, '"Era of global boiling has arrived", says UN chief as July set to be the hottest month on record', *the Guardian*, 27 July 2023.
8 See e.g. William MacAskill, *What We Owe the Future* (Oneworld, 2022).

9 'Paris summit on climate and finance ends without a deal on global shipping tax', *France 24*, 23 June 2023.
10 UNHRC General Comment No.36 (2018).
11 William Ophuls, *Immoderate Greatness: Why Civilizations Fail* (Create Space, 2012).
12 See e.g. 'Climate Change and the Radical Potential of Outrage to Advance the Frontiers of the Law', The Next 100 Years Project, Heilbron Lecture, 2022.
13 See e.g. Ben Batros and Tessa Khan, 'Thinking Strategically about Climate Litigation', from Part II – *Legal Strategy in Rights-Based Climate Litigation*, Cambridge University Press (online), 10 November 2022.
14 Statement given to the author.
15 *The State of the Netherlands (Ministers of Economic Affairs and Climate Policy) v Urgenda*, Supreme Court of the Netherlands, Civil Division, 19/00135.
16 *Juliana v United States*, 6:15-cv-01517.
17 Committee Member Helene Tigroudja, ochr.org, treaty body press releases, 23 September 2022.
18 See e.g. Supran and others, 'Assessing ExxonMobil's global warming projections', science.org, 13 January 2023, and Oliver Milman, 'Revealed: Exxon made "breathtakingly" accurate climate predictions in 1970s and 80s', *the Guardian*, 12 January 2023.
19 See Mathilda Mallinson, 'Crude justice: the Nigerians taking Shell to court', *Prospect*, June 2023 issue, 10 May 2023.
20 *Okpabi and Ors v Royal Dutch Shell Plc and Another* [2021] UKSC 3.
21 *Vereniging Milieudefensie v Royal Dutch Shell* [2021], Rechtbank Den Haag (District Court of The Hague), C/09/571932.
22 Mark Sweney, 'Shell "green" ad campaign banned in UK for being "likely to mislead"', *the Guardian*, 7 June 2023.

23 Dalia Palombo, 'The Future of the Corporation: the avenues for legal change', *Journal of the British Academy*, 10(s5), pp.43–86, 26 August 2022.
24 See stopecocide.earth
25 At the time of writing, Ukrainian authorities are marshalling evidence of such a crime by Russian forces. See e.g. Marc Santora, 'As Dead Dolphins Wash Ashore, Ukraine Builds a Case of Ecocide Against Russia', *The New York Times*, 17 August 2023.
26 Statement given to the author.
27 See *On Liberty*, p.124, and reaganlibrary.gov
28 Thatcher.org
29 David Conn, 'South Yorkshire interim police chief welcomes Orgreave Inquiry', *the Guardian*, 6 May 2016.
30 Otjc.org.uk
31 See Alison, Belinda, Helen Steel, Lisa and Naomi, *Deep Deception* (Penguin, 2022).
32 Rob Evans, Vikram Dodd and Paul Lewis, 'Police spying inquiry to examine targeting of UK black justice groups', *the Guardian*, 28 October 2020.
33 Rob Evans and Paul Lewis, 'Met pay compensation to man fathered by undercover officer', *the Guardian*, 7 October 2020.
34 'Getting to the truth of undercover policing and providing recommendations for the future', ucpi.org.uk
35 Covert Human Intelligence Sources (Criminal Conduct) Act 2021, c.4.
36 See e.g. 'Defenders of our Planet: Resilience in the Face of Restrictions', November 2021, civicus.net
37 See e.g. Priti Patel, 'They treat us all with contempt', *Mail Online*, 6 September 2020.
38 See e.g. Suella Braverman, 'A vote for Labour is literally a vote for the eco-zealots', X (formerly Twitter), 7 August 2023.

39 See Part 3 of the Police, Crime, Sentencing and Courts Act 2022 (c.32) and the Public Order Act 2023 (c.15).

40 See also Areeba Hamid and Will McCallum, 'You have adopted a bunker mentality': Greenpeace letter to Rishi Sunak, *the Guardian*, 10 August 2023.

41 'Arrested for doing my job', 9 November 2022, lbc.co.uk

42 The Public Order Act 2023 (Commencement No.1) (England and Wales) Regulations 2023, UK Statutory Instruments, 2023 No. 733 (c.38).

Conclusion

1 Baroness Hale of Richmond, DBE, PC, FBA, in *Ghaidan v Godin-Mendoza* [2004] UKHL 30.

Index